STARTING AND SUSTAINING

GENETIC SUPPORT GROUPS

STARTING AND SUSTAINING

GENETIC SUPPORT GROUPS

JOAN O. WEISS, M.S.W.

AND

JAYNE S. MACKTA

The Johns Hopkins University Press
Baltimore and London

The Johns Hopkins University Press
2715 North Charles Street
Baltimore, Maryland 21218-4319
The Johns Hopkins Press Ltd., London

Library of Congress Cataloging-in-Publication Data will be found
at the end of the book.
A catalog record for this book is available from the British Library.

ISBN 0-8018-5023-1   ISBN 0-8018-5264-1 (pbk.)

TO OUR CHILDREN,
WHO GOT US INVOLVED AND
TAUGHT US ABOUT CARING

Contents

Acknowledgments

We are grateful to our children and also to the untold number of exceptional people whose knowledge, commitment, and concern empower millions of people through genetic support groups. In particular, we thank the following leaders for freely sharing with us their wisdom and valuable insights: Melissa Aylstock, Klinefelter Syndrome and Associates; Hope Charkins, Treacher Collins Foundation; Jannine Cody, Chromosome 18 Registry and Research Society; Joan Edwards, Developmental Disabilities Prevention Program; Susan Fettes, Beckwith-Wiedemann Support Network; Marianne Haven, Pallister-Killian Family Support Group; Margaret Ieronimo, Foundation for Nager and Miller Syndromes; Abbey S. Meyers, National Organization for Rare Disorders; Sedra Schiffman, National Tay-Sachs and Allied Diseases Association; Betsy Wilson, Let's Face It; Mary Ann Wilson, Neurofibromatosis, Inc.; and Jody Zwain, Association for Children with Russell-Silver Syndrome.

We are equally appreciative of the many contributions by people who spoke to us or who wrote to us, many of whom wish to remain anonymous.

Our editor, Wendy Harris, also deserves thanks for her patience and faith in our ability to deliver a finished manuscript. Although we did not meet our many extended deadlines, we hope this book does come in time to spare group organizers some of the pains that inevitably come with starting and sustaining a genetic support group.

Finally, had we chosen a bumper sticker instead of a book as the preferred medium, we might have summed it up with an affirmation that never fails to charge the spirit: Progress, Not Perfection. We hope we are helping others to move in the right direction.

Introduction

What are some of the reasons that genetic support groups come into existence? Who initiates them? Is it the job of health care professionals to identify the need for support organizations and to initiate them? If so, should these professional leaders themselves have experienced a need for a support group? Should genetic support groups be started only by individuals who have specific disorders? And how does one go about assembling a group? Should the members of a genetic support group all have the same disorder, or can they offer support around issues that cross disability lines? Once a group is well established, what kind of structural framework is needed to keep it in existence?

These questions are all addressed in this book. There is substantial evidence that professionals and volunteers alike play an important role in the development and maintenance of a genetic support group, usually in close partnership. We hope to provide guidance and encouragement to those readers who, having recognized the need for a support group, are looking for direction in finding an effective way to start a group and in determining how to keep a group going—and growing stronger with time.

Although we discuss genetic support groups, much of what we write pertains to all support groups. Anyone interested in starting a support group and in seeing it survive and prosper, whether or not the group members have a genetic diagnosis, may find answers in this book. We intend this book to be a comprehensive and practical guide for individuals, families, and professionals motivated to start a new voluntary organization or to work with an existing one.

For the purposes of this book, we limit our definition of *consumers* to people who use genetic services. A genetic diagnosis involves the entire family, whether they know it or not and whether or not they wish to be involved. Therefore, this definition includes individuals who have been told that they have a genetic disorder, parents of a child who has been diagnosed as having a genetic disorder, and anyone with a family member who has a genetic disorder. Carriers (those individuals who have an altered gene that may be passed on to offspring but who do not have any symptoms themselves), carrier couples (couples who each have an altered gene that may be passed on to offspring), and women who have prenatal testing are all consumers in the broadest sense of genetic services, but they are not likely to volunteer their time to an organization involved with genetics unless they fit into one of the qualifying groups. As genetic information and new technologies become more accessible, our definition would not include all people who might need, or choose to avail themselves of, genetic services because that will eventually include everyone.

We define a *professional* as a person who has completed advanced studies in this specialized field and provides genetic services. Those who qualify are physicians, genetic counselors, nurses, social workers, educators, and research scientists, among others.

These definitions are based on common usage, but they give an incomplete picture. In fact, they can be considered labels, and they carry limitations. There is a line between the two categories that traditionally is not crossed. People in one category provide services; people in the other category receive these services. One charges for services; the other pays. One is the helper; the other is helped. One has power, be it in the form of knowledge or the ability to treat or cure; the other lacks power.

The need to label people, to classify them and put them into categories, reinforces barriers that separate families and professionals. In the world of genetics, professionals and consumers are not necessarily two separate groups of people. A genetic counselor may be the parent of a child with Down syndrome: a person with an inherited heart condition may be a physician. As researchers identify more problems with some connection to genetic makeup, the consumer group becomes larger.

Professionals and consumers may both be considered experts. In genetics, as in many fields, the life experience and knowledge of the consumer are essential to the good use of the scientific information and clinical experience of the professional. Now more than ever, there is a need to foster a partnership between professionals and families and to break down the barriers to communication. New scientific information is creating ethical dilemmas for consumers, professionals, and all of society. The decisions people must make in their personal and public lives will have a significant impact on the future.

Given the stake we all have in the future, it is critical that we take a hard look at definitions, expectations, and relationships. In essence, we need to unlock the tremendous potential of the partnership between families and professionals. The goal is to define roles so that they are inclusive, not exclusive—not to blur the traditional roles and responsibilities but to heighten awareness of the multiple facets of human existence. All human beings have something to contribute, something of value to share. We need to take the best of being a professional and being a consumer and forge an active alliance, through which interdependence and mutual respect shape attitudes and motivate people to help each other. A place to begin is the genetic support group, a setting where families and professionals work together with mutual respect and common purpose.

How to Use This Book

This is a "how to" book organized along traditional lines. If you start at the beginning and read through to the end, you can learn the basics of organizing and sustaining a genetic support group. There are samples to study and suggested guidelines to follow. A list of known genetic support groups can be found in Appendix A. Organizations with relevant expertise, many of which are referred to in the text, are listed in Appendix B.

Appendix C is a letter describing the success of one support group. The sources of information and quotations in the text are listed in the References. The Annotated Bibliography discusses additional sources of information on starting a group, group dynamics, fund-raising, and leadership. The Glossary contains definitions of genetic terminology.

As advocates for support groups, however, we believe that people learn best from others in similar circumstance who are willing to share personal experiences. Therefore, the anecdotal information gathered from genetic support group leaders might be the most valuable part of the book. In addition to advice, these ordinary people in extraordinary circumstances offer insights that are not easily indexed yet are certainly worth searching out. Beyond their words, you may recognize those elusive qualities that so often account for success when everything else would dictate failure. Read between the lines and you will see similarities: a passion to spare others pain they have known and a fierce determination to change one small piece of the world for the better.

Finally, everything included in this book, whether practical or personal, is our best effort at saving you from having to say, If I had only known about this before!

STARTING AND SUSTAINING

GENETIC SUPPORT GROUPS

–1–
The Evolution of Self-Help Organizations

The history of genetic support groups is rooted in the history of self-help organizations, which began years before people even knew that they or their children had genetic disorders.

A HISTORY OF SELF-HELP GROUPS

Beginning in the mid-1800s, immigrants arriving in the United States, faced with intolerance, overcrowded living conditions, and language problems, naturally turned to one another for solace. The so-called melting pot was, in reality, a standoff between assimilated Anglo-Saxon immigrants and the new arrivals, who tried to make a living despite unsanitary city slums or the isolation of rural communities. Structured self-help groups evolved as people searched for ways to overcome feelings of isolation and exclusion from the mainstream (Katz and Bender, 1990). Associations sprang up for non-English-speaking people having difficulty assimilating into their newly adopted country. A Greek community in Massachusetts formed the Pan-Hellenic Union. Russian and Polish Jews organized mutual help societies in the ghettos of major cities such as New York and Philadelphia. These support networks existed until immigration slowed at the onset of World War I and then began to spring up again with the successive waves of immigration that brought Hispanic, Asian, and Russian immigrants to this country.

Self-help groups began to take a different direction in the 1930s. In 1935, a drunken, down-and-out securities analyst from Wall Street met a former drinking pal who had joined the Calvary Episcopal Church in New York City, seeking a religious solution to his obsessive problem with alcohol. This reunion led to the formation of a group of recovering alcoholics at the Calvary Church and, eventually, to the formation of Alcoholics Anonymous (AA). The philosophy of the group was codified in the now-famous Twelve Steps used by AA as well as other self-help organizations. The inspirational words were written between 1935 and 1939 by AA co-founder Bill Wilson, the Wall Street dropout, along with other AA members (Powell, 1990).

Al-Anon was formed by wives of AA members in 1951 after they failed to find adequate support from other groups. Alateen was formed in 1957 for teenaged children of alcoholics. Today, the Al-Anon family groups include more than twenty-five thousand chapters. AA has more than forty thousand groups in a hundred countries (Borman, 1992).

Between 1950 and 1988, at least eighty new organizations requested AA's permission to use the copyrighted Twelve Step program (Katz and Bender, 1990). These self-help groups include Narcotics Anonymous (founded in 1953), Sexaholics Anonymous (founded in 1979), and Overeaters Anonymous (founded in 1980).

The appeal of the Twelve Step approach to self-help lies in its recognition of the power of guilt, individual feelings of isolation, a desire for repentance and reunion, and an eternal hope for inspiration after confession (Remine, Rice, and Ross, 1984). The members of groups motivated by the Twelve Steps seem preoccupied with a force that takes over their lives, whether it be alcohol or drugs, sex or food. To embark on the Twelve Step program, they begin by admitting that they cannot control their habit. They accept the need to replace their obsession with spiritual wholeness, by first taking personal inventory, then maintaining contact with a higher power, and finally offering help to those who still suffer (Kurtz, 1990).

Self-help organizations for individuals with physical and mental health concerns surfaced in the 1950s and 1960s, followed by special-purpose groups toward the end of the decade. Some of the larger and better-known self-help groups begun during that time are the National Hemophilia Foundation (1948), the Association for Retarded Citizens (1950), the Muscular Dystrophy Association of America (1950), the United Cerebral Palsy Association of America (1954), and the National Cystic Fibrosis Foundation (1957).

As the self-help movement has gained credibility, the focus of groups has become more diversified. MADD (Mothers Against Drunk Driving) has a strong political agenda. Groups such as Cocaine Anonymous have formed to help members fight specific forms of substance abuse. There are groups for people who are psychologically impaired, such as the National Alliance for the Mentally Ill (NAMI, founded in 1981). Most recently, clearinghouses have been formed on local, state, regional, and national levels that serve as resources for information and referral. They advocate for consumer groups and provide education for community members and professionals (Katz and Bender, 1990).

Clearinghouses and other forms of networking have been developed to promote the goals of self-help groups for rare disorders and to encourage greater public and professional awareness of their resources. The National Organization for Rare Disorders (NORD), established by Abbey Meyers in the mid-1980s, began as an informal federation of national voluntary health agencies, medical researchers, and individuals concerned about "orphan diseases" and "orphan drugs" (drugs not available from the pharmaceutical industry because it is not economically feasible to produce them in the small quantities needed). Rare disorders, most of which have a genetic basis, were identified as those affecting fewer than 200,000 persons in this country. The Orphan Drug Act of 1983 offered tax incentives to drug manufacturers to develop orphan drugs. Now, in addition to lobbying for the continuance of the Orphan Drug Act (but with certain amendments to avoid high prices for the consumer), NORD provides information in a computer-accessible database to both families and professionals, links together individuals with the same rare disorder, and advocates for research on and treatment of orphan diseases (Madara and Meese, 1990).

For the most part, the founders of health-related self-help groups are individuals who have family members afflicted with the disorder of concern. One example of an early self-help organization that fits this description is the Committee to Combat Huntington's Disease (now known as the Huntington's Disease Society of America). Huntington disease is a hereditary disorder of the central nervous system that does not usually express outward signs until adulthood, at which point abnormal tremors, dementia, and progressive physical deterioration occur, with death within ten to twenty-five years of the onset. Woody Guthrie, the famous folksinger, had Huntington disease. He was frequently taken to be drunk because of his stumbling gait and deteriorating physical and mental capacities. Shortly before her husband's death, Marjorie Guthrie located three other affected families and founded the Committee to Combat Huntington's Disease. She was appalled by the humiliation that her husband had to endure because of the lack of knowledge about his devastating genetic disorder and the resulting stigmatization by society. A true pioneer, she traveled across the country, meeting with parents, children, and friends of affected families. "I hear in their stories," she recounted, "remnants of my own" (Guthrie, 1979). Marjorie Guthrie is acknowledged as a leader in the self-help movement and continues to inspire those who assume responsibility for meeting unmet needs to help themselves, their families, and others in distress.

In other instances, groups have been founded by professionals working closely with consumers. The history of Parents Anonymous, founded in the early 1970s, illustrates the effectiveness of such a partnership. When Jolly K. expressed concern about herself and other potentially child-abusing parents, Dr. Leonard Leiber encouraged her to put an ad in the newspaper to reach others seeking the same kind of help. The ad read, "Parents, do you lose your cool with your kids? If so, call Jolly." Many calls came in, with requests for help in controlling rage toward children. Parents and professionals worked closely in establishing Parents Anonymous, which now has 1,500 chapters throughout the United States, Canada, and Europe (Borman, 1992).

In September 1987, the Office of the Surgeon General of the U.S. Public Health Service, under the leadership of Dr. C. Everett Koop, conducted a workshop, Self-Help and Public Health. The well-attended meeting, which attracted both consumers and professionals, emphasized the tremendous value of self-help groups and resulted in recommendations for increasing self-help activities. Dr. Koop stressed that health and human service providers alone could not ease the suffering of people who are physically or mentally ill or addicted. He underscored the need for a smooth working relationship between the orthodox, formal, well-recognized health care delivery system and self-help, mutual aid groups. A key recommendation from the workshop, which remains high on the list of seemingly impossible dreams, was to increase knowledge and change the attitudes and practices of health and human service providers by including information about self-help groups and their benefits in educational programs and in practice settings.

As a direct result of the workshop, federal health and human service agencies began to incorporate self-help in their policies and fund-raising priorities. When the National Council on Self-Help and Public Health was established in 1987, there was national recognition that the process of people coming together to help one another was legitimate and useful. The council was funded by the Maternal and Child Health Bureau to establish the National Project for Self-Help Groups, which has as one of its major goals increasing public and professional awareness of the benefits of self-help groups. As a result of heightened awareness, recently formed support groups, such as those for persons with HIV infection and those for families involved in child abuse and neglect, have been publicly recognized and praised for their positive effect in behavioral changes as well as for their encouragement of the sharing of anxieties and fears (Hedrick, Isenberg, and Martini, 1992).

A HISTORY OF GENETIC SUPPORT GROUPS

Increasingly, self-help groups are being established both by those affected by genetic disorders and by concerned health care providers such as genetic counselors and social workers. To date, more than 250 genetic voluntary organizations are listed in the *Directory of National Genetic Voluntary Organizations and Related Resources* (Alliance of Genetic Support Groups, 1995). These organizations, multiplying so rapidly, try to keep pace as science races to identify particular genes and perfect the technology to diagnose, treat, and prevent genetic disorders. They are an integral part of the larger self-help movement, which has been gaining in strength and numbers as human needs outpace the availability of appropriate, accessible, and affordable services.

A genetic support group can serve one or more of the following purposes:

- Address special needs that are not being met elsewhere.

- Provide mutual help.
- Educate professionals and the public about a specific disorder.
- Stimulate and fund research.

Three well-established organizations for individuals and families with genetic disorders illustrate the different purposes such groups can serve. One is Little People of America (LPA), which was founded by an actor, Billy Barty, in 1957. He was one of twenty-one individuals of short stature from nine states who assembled in Reno, Nevada, to set out their plan for a support organization. They then contacted hospitals, schools, and even jails to attract potential members (Ablon, 1984). Thirty-nine years later, LPA has more than four thousand members from all over the United States and a strong link to similar groups in Canada, Europe, and Asia.

As is true of many voluntary organizations, the goals of the LPA are reflected in its by-laws: "The purpose of LPA is to assist its members in adjusting to the social and physical problems of life caused by their small stature through mutual assistance and the personal examples by each of its members." These by-laws also record that LPA was organized out of concern about the need of short-statured persons to become useful members of society through adequate education, employment, and social adjustment. A second reason for the formation of this group was to help the public recognize that the magnitude of any physical limitation is a function of the attitudes of both small and average-sized individuals (Barty, 1982).

LPA is unique in that it is run by the affected individuals themselves rather than by parents or professionals. Although its original orientation was primarily social, in recent years the organization has incorporated educational and psychosocial symposia into its annual conventions. The national group now has a parents' group, which holds meetings each morning at the national convention, in addition to a young adults' group, a teenagers' group, and an adoption committee, which works with child-placing agencies all over the country. There is, in addition, an extremely active sports committee, which arranges competitive athletic events both within LPA and at international Special Olympic events. All in all, LPA has become increasingly successful in meeting the goals established in that first meeting in Reno.

The second organization is the National Tay-Sachs and Allied Diseases Association (NTSAD), which was founded in 1957 by parents committed to the eradication of this rare disease and more than twenty related disorders. Tay-Sachs disease is a progressive, debilitating disorder that affects infants primarily of Central and Eastern European Jewish descent and results in early death. The mother of a child with Tay-Sachs disease makes a compelling case for support groups: "We found that when Susan was born in 1970, the doctors knew almost as little about her condition as we did. Also, the information we found in textbooks was severely limited. We felt isolated. We needed to know what to expect. The doctors worried about us getting information from other parents. We searched for a group."

In the late 1960s, researchers discovered the cause of Tay-Sachs disease and were then able to develop a simple blood test to identify carriers of the Tay-Sachs gene. With a specific population to test, it became possible and practical to launch a community education program, which led to the first mass screening to identify carriers, in 1971 in Maryland. Group activities shifted from parents supporting each other and raising funds to seek a treatment and cure to public and professional education about the disease as well as screening and prevention programs. Now the emphasis has shifted again, and efforts are directed at urging professionals to advise couples to be tested before pregnancy. The organization also supports a growing network of parents. Support is provided via telephone to more than 380 families widely separated geographically. The latest challenge to the organization is the identification of several families with young adults affected with a late-onset variant, whose needs are very different from those of families whose children die within the first few years of life.

The third organization was founded in 1978, when a patient with neurofibromatosis (NF), the most common genetic neurological disorder, took the initiative and reached out to others for help. Together, members of the group formulated goals, such as increasing research and improving public education and support services. They formed a medical advisory board and raised start-up funds. Their small group wrote a fact sheet and a newsletter and contacted the media and medical schools nationwide about their organization.

In the wake of widespread publicity about a play called *The Elephant Man,* the phone never stopped ringing in the NF apartment/office. Although John Merrick, the patient about whom the play was written, turned out to have had a different severe disorder, possibly in addition to neurofibromatosis, the publicity nonetheless focused attention on the support group. The inaccurate diagnosis of Merrick, however, contributed to a public misconception about NF that continues to plague many individuals with the disorder, who are stigmatized by the implication that they resemble the Elephant Man.

Eventually, NF chapters were formed throughout the United States. Literature about NF was printed, substantial contributions were made to the NF Research Fund, legislation focusing attention on NF was introduced in Congress, and an executive office was established in New York City. From the mutual sharing of concerns by a few individuals and families, a highly visible and successful genetic support organization has emerged. By the late 1980s, two other national support groups for neurofibromatosis had been formed: Neurofibromatosis, Inc., and NF 2, Inc. In 1990, the gene for NF 1, the more common form of neurofibromatosis, was discovered. By 1993, the gene for the rarer form, known as NF 2, had also been found.

Several national voluntary genetic organizations are the result of mergers of two or more support groups with interests in common. The Huntington's Disease Society of America (HDSA) was created by the merger of the Huntington's Disease Foundation of America and the National Huntington's Disease Association. The Committee to Combat Huntington's Disease, established in 1967, was the predecessor of them all.

Many smaller networks of genetic support groups have been developing in recent years. The MPS Society (1974), for example, includes metabolic disorders such as Hurler and Hunter syndromes and is strengthened by covering several rare genetic disorders within the one organization. With the help of the Alliance of Genetic Support Groups, a new support group was formed in 1992 for parents of children with exceptionally rare chromosomal deletions, called Chromosome Deletion Outreach Network. If it were not for this organization, many of these parents would not be able to find other parents with whom to share mutual concerns and resources.

Even in the 1980s, however, many parents of children with genetic disorders still felt helpless and alone. From the diary of a mother whose daughter died of Sandhoff disease eight days before her second birthday:

I was astounded by most of the doctors and nurses I contacted and their lack of information and help. I just assumed that they kept abreast of organizations and aids for people in our situation . . . and I was shocked to learn that they don't. Even many of the obvious organizations I contacted were of little or no help. Therefore, we had to do all the legwork in seeking assistance . . . and that was about as simple as trying to bake a cake without any ingredients on hand! I had to learn the hard way, not by choice. And now that I know what I know, I want to pass on all this knowledge to other mothers seeking help, but I don't know how to go about it. No one should have to feel that helpless.

The challenge of finding others to help or to be helped by is intensified for many individuals with genetic disorders and their families if the incidence of their specific disorder is low. It is extraordinary, however, how one family can locate others once they begin the outreach process. The founder of the Association for Children with Russell-Silver Syndrome thought her son was the only child in the country with the rare disorder. Not until she and her husband formed the association did she discover that another baby with the syndrome had been born in the same hospital just a few months before her son. They began with a list of seventeen families identified through NORD and, within three years, had located almost three hundred families all around the world.

In 1983, the Mid-Atlantic Regional Human Genetics Network, with the combined support of the March of Dimes Birth Defects Foundation and the Maternal and Child Health Bureau, conducted a national symposium, Genetic Disorders and Birth Defects in Families and Society: Toward Interdisciplinary Understanding. Out of this meeting, held in Baltimore, came the recommendation for the development of a coalition to legitimize individual genetic support groups and help them become a unified force with a common purpose. Such a coalition, it was proposed, would link voluntary genetic groups to the scientific and research communities, further public education about genetics and genetic disorders, and provide a structure for unified political action (Weiss, Bernhardt, and Paul, 1984).

The next national conference that took place for those interested in genetic support groups was called Self-Help Groups for Genetic Blood Disorders. This conference illustrated the importance of developing self-help groups for families of individuals with sickle-cell anemia and related disorders such as hemophilia. The meeting, held in Washington, D.C., in 1985, was sponsored by the Division of Blood Diseases and Resources at the National Institutes of Health. Most participants were African American self-helpers. They demonstrated ways in which minority members can be engaged in organizations, such as those represented by the conference participants (Powell, 1987).

As a result of the recommendations from the 1983 Baltimore symposium, and again with joint funding from the March of Dimes and the Maternal and Child Health Bureau, more than ninety voluntary genetic organizations sent representatives to Washington in 1985 to another national symposium. This one, sponsored by Georgetown University and the Johns Hopkins Medical Institutions, focused on identifying common concerns of genetic support groups and strengthening a partnership between families and the professionals involved with these groups (Weiss et al., 1986). This time a recommendation was made to form a consortium of voluntary genetic support groups to move forward in expressing common aims.

A planning committee of seven "consumers" and two professionals met in August 1985 to design the administrative structure of the proposed coalition, develop goals and objectives, and identify ways of funding this federation of genetic support groups. Today, the Alliance of Genetic Support Groups is composed of more than 210 organizational members as well as hundreds of concerned individuals, both consumers and professionals. A flourishing coalition, the alliance serves as a forum for new ideas and strategies, as an information resource and clearinghouse, and as an agent for change in the area of genetic services. By strengthening collaboration and communication between consumers and providers of genetic services, the alliance seeks to increase national and regional awareness about genetic disorders, improve the availability and accessibility of high-quality genetic services, and enhance education about the needs of affected individuals and families. Its staff, board of directors, and committee members network among voluntary, professional, and governmental organizations concerned with genetic services.

The Alliance of Genetic Support Groups links individuals and families with genetic support groups and refers them to appropriate professionals for genetic services. Other functions include the publication of the monthly *Alert* and the distribution of the brochures of

Coalitions like the Alliance of Genetic Support Groups play a valuable role in focusing national awareness on the programs of hundreds of individual groups. (Alliance of Genetic Support Groups)

member groups at national professional and consumer meetings. Gaps in services are identified by such means as surveys of members (Black and Weiss, 1988). Then strategies are employed to develop needed services, such as the publication of *Health Insurance Resource Guide* (1992) and *National Directory of Voluntary Genetic Organizations and Related Resources* (1995).

As new technologies are developed and information about genetics increases, the public needs more and more assistance in gaining access to information. Calls pour in on the Alliance's toll-free telephone number. Individuals affected by genetic disorders, families and friends, students, librarians, and a wide range of professionals want information about specific disorders, genetic support groups, and genetics in general. Many seek information about the potential impact of mapping the human genome and about genetic screening and testing. In response, with the encouragement of the American Society of Human Genetics and the National Institutes of Health, the alliance published *Guidelines for Informed Consent for Participants in Genetic Research Studies.*

The demands on genetic support groups to serve as a resource to the public will continue to grow. Beyond meeting the ever-changing needs of individual members and the needs of the organization itself, groups will have to find new and effective ways of educating the public. Not until a true partnership with the professional health care community exists, however, will genetic support groups be able to participate fully in this critical process.

WHY ARE SUPPORT GROUPS SO SUCCESSFUL?

What accounts for the tremendous growth in the self-help movement? According to the late Dr. Leonard D. Borman (1992), there are four major factors: (1) the erosion of the extended family unit, which formerly served as a support network; (2) populist movements within which women, African Americans, and persons with disabling conditions, among others, have been encouraged to assert their right to make decisions that affect them directly; (3) a recognition of the increasing hazards of lifestyles overrun by such conditions as addiction or depression; and (4) limited professional services for those in need of them. Increased mobility is another factor: people on the move have no time to establish roots or to find support in familiar surroundings.

The absence of extended families has created a void that is being filled with professionals—people trained and paid to offer help. To counter the depersonalization that comes with dealing with big institutions and their accompanying bureaucracy, people seek out others who share their personal concerns, searching for emotional support as well as information. They turn to people who live with similar problems and who have gained knowledge through experience instead of, or in addition to, education.

More and more, people are becoming involved in their own care by belonging to mutual help groups. Networking of this sort is particularly appealing to those needing a shift in social roles, such as recovering alcoholics or new parents. These natural helping networks often evolve into voluntary organizations whose members want to regain a sense of control over their lives, their resources, and even the policy decisions that affect them and their loved ones.

Once others affected by the same disorder are found, families begin to address their most pressing needs. Without formal planning, most groups begin to engage in similar activities.

- legitimizing members' feelings
- providing a comfortable environment
- helping defeat feelings of isolation
- stimulating change
- providing a link between consumers and health care providers
- empowering individuals to speak out
- helping members become a unified force with a unified purpose

Members share information and resources with one another. Some groups offer direct services to their members, for example, by providing them with peer support or needed rehabilitative devices. They disseminate information in an effort to help eliminate misdiagnoses and reduce the amount of time other families might have to wait for a confirmed diagnosis. Organizational brochures, fact sheets, and newsletters contain information for both public and professional consumption. Leaders network with related organizations and join broad coalitions as part of a strategy to reach a larger audience with information about their particular disorder and their group. They list organizational information with national clearinghouses and in reference directories.

Genetic support groups rely on empathetic professionals, particularly those who serve on professional advisory boards, to carry their materials and their mission to meetings where consumers have no platform. The groups send mailings to individual physicians and large medical centers. They post announcements in supermarkets. Some have members who volunteer to speak to medical students. Others testify before commissions and legislative bodies. They sponsor symposiums and run conferences at which families and professionals can interact. They assist in locating families to participate in research and often provide initial funding for genetic research projects. They monitor all work that could provide them or future families with a breakthrough.

Because they usually focus on a single disorder, genetic support groups tend to have up-to-the-minute information on specific research as well as treatments and therapies. Collectively, members qualify as

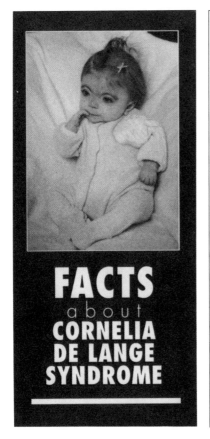

A brochure may be the first contact a person has with a genetic support group, and both the design and the text should reflect the personality as well as the priorities of the group. Many groups choose to use a photograph on the cover of the brochure, to connect the reader immediately with the human dimension of the disorder. (Cornelia de Lange Syndrome Foundation and Osteogenesis Imperfecta Foundation)

experts when it comes to recognizing symptoms and as knowledgeable referral sources for genetic counseling and other genetic services. They know all too well that with the medical diagnosis come a host of human problems that do not readily fit into the job description of any one professional. As a consequence of on-the-job training, they often gain knowledge regarding day-to-day care that is not taught to clinicians.

Such accumulated knowledge is put to good use. By increasing public awareness about a particular genetic disorder, these groups often play an important role in advocating change in public opinion and law. Many groups work to educate the public about a disorder in an effort to prevent its occurrence, if possible, or to publicize the availability of genetic screening, if available. Some groups provide important services to newly diagnosed families and are there for grieving families as well. A sickle cell group has developed treatment guidelines for distribution to hospital emergency rooms. The National Tay-Sachs and Allied Diseases Association has translated its brochures into Russian in a concerted effort to reach the thousands of Jewish immigrants who have arrived in the United States from the former Soviet Union. Little People of America has established an adoption committee, linking those parents who wish to place their children for adoption with dwarfed couples who have been approved as adoptive couples by licensed child-placing agencies.

Genetic support groups work hard to be accessible to the public. Those that can afford it maintain toll-free telephone numbers. They invest in costly publications and public service announcements. They develop slide shows, videotapes, and traveling displays, all to carry their message of hope and help to the public.

There are some areas of concern where groups need greater numbers and sustained momentum for impact. Genetic support groups consisting of parents or families of individuals affected by genetic disorders often have the responsibility of both caregiving and running an organization. The demands of giving help when you need it yourself can be overwhelming. Every success means broader visibility and increased demands for resources and expertise. In areas such as health care financing or improving the accessibility and affordability of high-quality genetic services, groups have joined coalitions like the National Organization for Rare Disorders and the Alliance of Genetic Support Groups to strengthen their impact.

By banding together, genetic support groups often have been part of successful advocacy movements, such as the enactment of the Orphan Drug Act and the Americans with Disabilities Act. They also have begun joint efforts to educate the public about the uniqueness of families affected by genetic conditions. Together these groups can emphasize the needs of individuals with genetic disorders by offering them a platform from which to get out messages of frustration to the public as well as the health care community.

— 2 —

Why People Seek
Genetic Support
Groups

• Sam, a boy with a severe genetic disorder called Treacher Collins syndrome, was featured on a national television show in the spring of 1988. In the weeks that followed, families from all over the United States contacted a Boston clinic mentioned in the program to reach the boy's parents. It was soon apparent that these families needed to form a network with other families to share mutual concerns and to exchange information.

• When Jane was born, the attending physician told her parents that she had Down syndrome and that probably the best plan would be for them to institutionalize her. The couple, who were in their early twenties, thought that only older parents had children with Down syndrome. They did not know what to expect and were terribly frightened. If only they could talk to other parents who could advise them on what to do!

• Jimmy, a fifteen-year-old with dwarfism, had had many average-sized friends until the boys his age began to date. Suddenly, he felt left out. He became acutely aware of how different he looked and was afraid of rejection by his former pals and the girls he longed to date. Could anyone else know the agony he was experiencing? He felt that his tall parents could never understand.

- Carol was a very tall, thin paralegal with Marfan syndrome. The thirty-year-old woman faced cardiac surgery to avoid possible rupture of her aorta, which had increased dramatically in size. Although a member of the National Marfan Foundation since she was nineteen, Carol needed a special kind of support, which she sought in a summer symposium focusing on decisions about surgery. In one place at one time, she was able to speak to several people who had already been through this surgical procedure, which can be as threatening as the rupture it is performed to prevent.

The unique benefits of support and empathy that come from one's peers, from those who understand from personal experience, are irreplaceable and explain why people such as those described above seek the help of a support group.

- The Treacher Collins Family Network was established in August 1988 in response to the need assessed by the Boston clinic that had been mentioned on the television program. Sam's parents agreed to organize and develop the network, which now acts as a central resource to link together persons affected by this genetic disorder. Families share concerns, exchange information about methods for coping with this rare and complex syndrome, and plan educational strategies and support for research.

- Jane's parents tried to use their friends and family as a sounding board for their feelings about institutionalization versus bringing their baby home. What they really needed was to draw on the strength and support of parents who had been through similar soul searching, people who could understand and tell them what it was like to have a child with Down syndrome. The hospital social worker introduced them to a couple who had a five-year-old with Down syndrome. The couple urged Jane's parents to attend a local parent support group meeting, where other parents provided them with factual information about children with Down syndrome that helped them decide whether or not to keep Jane at home.

- One day, Jimmy saw a notice in his local newspaper that a meeting of Little People of America was to take place at a nearby park. He had heard about the organization but had felt no connection. Jimmy went to the gathering at the park, and that first meeting was quite frightening to him. He thought he looked more "normal" than other dwarfed individuals. He looked at the other short-statured people and thought, "I'm not like them. I don't walk like them. I'm taller than they are." But the shock of that first encounter gave way to the realization that he was lonely. Perhaps the group could help him to gain friends he could look straight in the eye, knowing that they understood what it was like to be left out because of one's size. Through the group activities, Jimmy began to accept himself the way he was and to recognize that he was not the only one in the world who might not date an average-sized girl. He soon met a fourteen-year-old girl with dwarfism, whom he began taking to school events.

• Carol had the benefit of belonging to an organization started by physicians and families who saw the need for a support group. Group members believed that they were getting good medical care, but they still had many concerns, such as societal attitudes toward their physical appearance, limitations placed on their participation in sports, and the threat of severe heart problems. Hundreds of families now eagerly await the medical and social bulletins of the National Marfan Foundation and look forward to getting together at chapter and national conferences.

In each instance, a genetic support group offered a special service that could not have been duplicated by even the best-intentioned health care provider or loving family member.

Genetic support groups are different from other types of support groups in that they usually represent not only individuals with a specific problem but also family members who are at risk themselves, who may be affected at a later time, or who may be carriers of the mutated gene. Since genetic disorders are often intergenerational as well as familial, these voluntary organizations can involve grand-parents in addition to the affected individuals, their children, siblings, and parents. In addition, a genetic support group takes into account the extreme variability of symptoms the genetic disorder may display and the variety of ways in which individuals and family members are affected by it.

THE ROLE OF GENETIC COUNSELING

There is general agreement that the timing and sensitivity of making referrals to a genetic support group are crucial. For instance, meeting someone else with the same genetic condition is not always helpful for people who have just received a genetic diagnosis (Silverman, 1992). During this time, which can be filled with confusion and anguish, genetic counseling can be extremely valuable, to help people understand and begin coping with a genetic condition.

As defined by the American Society of Human Genetics in 1975, genetic counseling is considered to be "a communication process which deals with the human problems associated with the occurrence or risk of recurrence of a genetic disorder in a family." Genetic counseling can be offered by individuals who are certified as genetic counselors. These specialists have completed advanced training in genetics programs with a counseling component. Genetic counseling can also be given by physicians, nurses, or social workers who have had special training in genetics. They may be part of a clinic team or may be affiliated with a private enterprise, such as a laboratory or research facility. There are also some genetic counselors in private practice.

A professional with specialized knowledge, a genetic counselor addresses questions and concerns raised by persons having an inherited disorder or trait. He or she provides information to help patients make decisions related to having a genetic disorder, being a carrier of an altered gene, or having offspring who may inherit the altered gene. In addition to helping individuals and couples understand their genetic diagnosis, if there is one, the counselor provides information to assist them in making informed decisions about family planning according to their personal values and goals.

Most genetic counseling takes place in genetics centers located in urban settings within large medical centers. Some of these have satellite outreach programs to assist people who live in less-populated areas. Generally, referrals come from physicians or family members. It has been documented, however, that genetic support groups often refer members to the genetics clinic either because they have never received genetic counseling or because they or a family member have had a crisis associated with a particular genetic disorder (Black and Weiss, 1988).

People need genetic counseling for many reasons. There may be a family history of a specific or suspected genetic disorder. A couple may know that they are first cousins or close relatives, or they may have similar ethnic backgrounds (such as African American or Eastern European Jewish). A woman may have had multiple miscarriages or stillbirths or be infertile; she may have been exposed to a drug, radiation, or alcohol during the pregnancy.

Likewise, people want prenatal diagnoses for many reasons. Perhaps a previous child has a chromosomal problem, or one parent is a known carrier of a chromosomal abnormality. Perhaps the mother is thirty-five or older, or the parents are particularly anxious about the outcome of the pregnancy. Others who might seek a prenatal diagnosis include parents who are suspected or identified carriers of an autosomal recessive disorder, a parent who is affected by an autosomal dominant disorder, a mother who is a carrier of an X-linked recessive disorder, or a parent who has a first- or second-degree relative with a neural tube defect (e.g., spina bifida).

Genetic counselors are trained to help the people they see to understand the facts about genetics in general as well as the specific genetic disorder with which they are concerned. They also enable patients to come to their own decisions about such important matters as whether or not to have prenatal testing or to have another child. Genetic counselors explain available options and should support the patient's decision (March of Dimes Birth Defects Foundation, 1992). Their role is to help patients choose the course of action that seems appropriate to them in view of their risk and their family goals.

The genetic counseling process varies from center to center but basically involves gathering information, a physical examination, establishing a diagnosis, counseling, and follow-up (see Scott, 1988).

---

1. *Gather information*
   Previous records, family photos
   Family history
   Pregnancy, delivery, neonatal history
   Medical history
   Growth and development

2. *Physical examination*

3. *Establish a diagnosis*
   Review history
   Diagnostic testing
   Review the literature, consult with colleagues

4. *Genetic counseling*
   Explain the diagnosis, etiology, prognosis
   Discuss treatment/management
   Clarify recurrence risks
   Review options
   Assist in decision making, adjustment to diagnosis

5. *Followup*
   Make appropriate referrals
   Communicate with primary care providers
   Provide a written summary to the family
   Suggest extended family studies as needed

The genetic counselor takes a family history to determine whether the patient, spouse, parents, grandparents, or siblings have or had any genetic problems. A family tree, called a pedigree, is then constructed to see if the individual seeking help is, in fact, at risk for a genetic disorder. An accurate diagnosis is sought to help determine if the individual has a genetic condition that can be passed on to future generations and to find out the prognosis, treatment, and management.

The patient is given a physical examination, as are any family members who may provide significant data. The genetic counselor arranges for laboratory tests such as blood tests, when indicated, to rule out or identify chromosomal problems. He or she then puts all the information together as the basis for discussing the findings and considering what they mean for the individual or the family.

The person or couple being counseled should feel comfortable asking questions until everything is clear. A written report of the visit, including a summary of the diagnosis, the genetic counseling, the recommended treatment, and the plans for follow-up, should be sent to both the patient and the primary physician. It may be recommended that other family members found to be at risk for the genetic disorder be contacted for evaluation and genetic counseling.

Follow-up counseling should be made available to the patient and family. Because it is often difficult to absorb all the information in one or two visits to the genetics clinic, return visits over a period of time may be necessary until all the information is fully understood. There may also be new genetic situations in the family to interpret. The genetic counselor can also refer the patient and family, at their request, to community resources such as other medical specialists, educational specialists, or family support groups.

Although genetic counselors should be knowledgeable about recent advancements in genetic technology, testing, treatment, and resources, they are being challenged by the explosion of new genetic information. For example, along with the mapping of our genes, more and more genetic tests are becoming available. A carrier test for cystic fibrosis has been developed. Tests are available to find out whether a person has the gene for Huntington disease before symptoms are apparent. As more genes and genetic markers are located and genetic information continues to expand, the questions and concerns also expand. Consequently, individual counselors will have to know more, and there will be an even greater need for additional trained genetic counselors because there will be more anxious people.

COPING WITH FEELINGS IS PART OF THE PROCESS

Genetic support groups can be viewed as partners with genetics professionals in that they too attempt to help the individual or family make the best possible adjustment. No matter how skilled the genetic counselor and the rest of the genetics team may be, they cannot offer the kind of help that comes from those who have lived the experience themselves.

Although most individuals and families adjust to and cope well with a genetic disorder, they do so with a fair amount of heartache and struggle. One common reaction shared by many individuals with genetic disorders or parents of an affected child, particularly when first receiving the diagnosis, is to feel isolated and out of control. The specter of huge medical bills, tough questions from family and friends, and the prospect of lifelong caretaking responsibilities can become a nightmare. It seems as if everyone else is happy and going about the normal routines of life. Questions about the future resonate through long, restless nights. Perhaps the most pressing is how to get through the next hour.

The need for support may be most crucial around the time of diagnosis. It may level off for some time and then reemerge during periods of transition or crisis. Whether needs lessen over time or not, they certainly change.

Sedra Schiffman began her ongoing struggle almost thirty years ago when her infant daughter was diagnosed with Tay-Sachs disease:

> While our daughter Caron was still at home, effort focused on finding the energy, time, and skills to care for her and the rest of my family—a more than full-time commitment and challenge. Then came the awareness that caring for her at home was becoming a twenty-four-hour-a-day activity. And even with a twenty-four-hour commitment, I was rapidly coming to the understanding that I didn't possess the training or skills to handle the complex medical problems that were arising day by day with increasing frequency. With no help, no home nursing or medical personnel or other regular assistance, it was becoming clear that some alternative plan had to be at least considered. We looked, researched, and finally made the decision that hospitalizing Caron was the best option available to us. And so we did. To this day, while intellectually I understand all the reasons and reasoning that went into that decision, I still feel as if on February 7, 1969, I abandoned my child. That awful sense, along with the huge vacuum that was created in my life when the burden and time commitment of caring for her were whisked away, left me with an intense need, drive, maybe obsession: even if there were nothing I could do to save my own child, I had to do *something*, find some way to fight back, or if not fight back, at least to move forward.

In 1969, Sedra helped start, and became the first president of, the Delaware Valley Chapter of National Tay-Sachs and Allied Diseases Association. Over the years, she has served as national president for two terms and chaired every major committee on the chapter and national levels. She continued to maintain a high degree of involvement while studying to become a genetic counselor.

For many people like Sedra, knowledge leads to action and is a powerful weapon in the battle to survive. The founder of a support group called K. S. and Associates for families with Klinefelter syndrome, a genetic alteration occurring only in males and identified by the presence of extra X chromosomes, vividly recalls the outrage she felt when being refused information about the condition affecting her eight-year-old son: "We were seen by a genetic counselor, who told my husband and me that while she did have information on Klinefelter syndrome, it was not written for laymen. She would not share any medical articles in her possession. She also said she wouldn't be able to put us in contact with any other families because of privacy issues. I have always hated being told no. I hate being talked down to. The day after the counseling visit, I was at the medical library with change in hand for the copy machine. I will admit that I didn't like what I read; a lot of it was scary, but that was my choice."

The mother of a young adult with neurofibromatosis type 1, a common neurological genetic disorder that can cause tumors to form on the nerves anywhere in the body at any time, explained her similar drive to learn as much as possible about the disease: "I do not like surprises, so I try to keep up with the research being conducted in NF." She also wanted her son to be in the position to receive treatment as soon as it is available. Knowledge, therefore, helped restore her sense of control and ease feelings of powerlessness.

The amount of psychological pain and suffering experienced by persons with genetic disorders and family members varies from individual to individual as well as from situation to situation. All families coping with chronic illness or early death suffer some degree of anguish for many of the same reasons. Upon learning that their child has a life-threatening or lifelong illness, some parents feel numb, confused, and helpless. Others are initially distrustful of the diagnosis and seek additional opinions. Still others immediately look for someone to blame. Some seek professional help. Some people look for support and comfort; others retreat inward.

Common to all is the initial shock that presages upheaval and irreversible change. Whether there is a definitive diagnosis or only the unsettling knowledge that "something is wrong," it is necessary to go through an actual grieving process (Kubler-Ross, 1969). Grieving for the loss of a dream that includes having a perfect child, good health, or living happily ever after, everyone needs to go through stages, which can occur in any order: shock and denial, anger and resentment, bargaining and guilt, sadness and depression, and, finally, acceptance and coping with reality. Individuals move back and forth within these stages.

The mother of a daughter with severe facial disfigurement admits that, at first, she wanted to go home from the hospital and hide, pretending that she didn't have a baby at all. She wanted to start over. After a short time, this mother began to examine her own feelings and realized that she was very concerned about other people's reaction to her child's appearance. Once she accepted her initial feelings of guilt, fear, and shame, she moved beyond caring what other people might think. In the process of becoming proud of her child, she developed a much stronger sense of herself.

The mother of a young adult with Down syndrome found the values instilled during her childhood prepared her to cope with the unexpected challenges her son's condition presented: "I was taught to help with chores, learned good values, and the meaning of accepting one's lot in life by making the best of whatever you had." Not everyone, however, can make lemons into lemonade. Many factors affect an individual's response, including previous experience with people who have a progressive illness or chronic disability, financial circumstances, and availability of support systems.

A general lack of knowledge about rare diseases, many of which are genetic, can sometimes add extra layers of devastation. For example, parents of children with osteogenesis imperfecta, a disorder that results in multiple bone breaks, have been accused of child abuse. One couple's baby was taken away from them when she was two weeks old because she fractured her arm: "They took her away from us and put her in foster care. Our baby was already eighteen months old before she was allowed to come back to us. We were unable to pay for a dedicated attorney. We were submitted to traumatic humiliation, prohibitive court costs, and, most importantly, unbearable separation from the baby we loved. They just didn't understand. . . . They won't ever understand our devastation" (OIF, *1990–91 Annual Report,* p. 6). Who else but someone with the same experience can imagine the degree to which guilt felt about causing one's child any kind of pain is compounded when the parent of a youngster with osteogenesis imperfecta breaks the child's brittle bones in the course of routine care?

Along with guilt, feelings about "burden" have a double edge. Affected individuals feel guilty for being a burden; family members may fear or resent the burdens that are part of the responsibility of caring for a person with a disability or chronic illness. Anxiety and fear of the unknown can become constant companions. In a deeply personal and revealing article entitled "The Something That Happened before I Was Born," Marsha Saxton (n.d.) recalls the dread that engulfed her as a child when hearing the news of impending leg surgery. Director of the Project on Women and Disability, based in Boston, Marsha has spina bifida, a spinal cord defect caused by a combination of genetic and other factors. "I recall sitting in the rocker, my mother crying. I felt as if a big hand were reaching into our family to pluck me out. My parents seemed powerless; there was nothing they could do to prevent my leaving. I remember, too, how little attention was paid to the surgery happening to help my legs work better. At the time, especially when I was young, that just seemed like a ruse to obscure what I knew was really true: my body was defective and so I had to be punished."

The public knows relatively little about genetics and the genetic transmission of conditions or diseases, and less about the various factors that can affect them. The names of most genetic disorders are difficult to pronounce, hard to remember, and even harder to spell. Consequently, families of an individual with a genetic disorder can be subject to additional stresses resulting from their own lack of understanding. The parents of an affected child may feel defective. They can be plagued by agonizing questions such as, What did I do wrong? Am I being punished for something I did or did not do? Affected individuals ask many of the same questions and can harbor troubling and distorted images of themselves and family members.

Abbey Meyers, parent of three children with Tourette syndrome, a widely misunderstood neurological disorder characterized by involuntary tics and noises, clearly recalls her anguish as a young mother: "My oldest son couldn't sit still and be quiet, which was the only prerequisite to passing kindergarten. There was something obviously wrong with him, but no one knew what. As his involuntary movements and noises grew worse over the years, we punished him, but that didn't do any good. So we punished ourselves because it must be our fault, but that didn't do any good either."

It is natural to look for the cause for what appears to have "gone wrong." Parents may blame themselves for poor prenatal care, exposure to environmental risks, medications, infection, and so on, or even such imagined causes as negative thoughts about childbearing during pregnancy. Denial is not uncommon. Spouses may blame each other for not having shared genetic information before marriage. Perhaps the ultimate hurt comes when one spouse declares, "It's not on my side!"

Grandparents may carry the double burden of passing the gene to their children, who then pass it on to the next generation. Affected adults who discover their condition only after the birth of a more severely affected child may blame themselves for having passed on the gene to their child.

Unaffected siblings have their own issues and exhibit a range of reactions. These include feelings of guilt that they are not affected, fear that they may become affected, hostility toward the affected brother or sister, who is perceived to get preferential treatment, and jealousy of the attention to the sick or medically fragile sibling's demands. Some adolescents and even adults resent an affected sibling and feel embarrassed to be seen in public with a brother or sister who has an obvious physical difference or who "acts out."

Because of the stigmatizing nature of many genetic disorders, affected individuals and families may continue to feel alone and different until they meet others with the same genetic condition. If a condition is rare as well as genetic, it is common for a family not to know anyone else with the same condition. Many are shocked to discover a prior incidence in their own family. After a diagnosis, it is not uncommon to learn that some relative, perhaps never mentioned before, had the same disorder or at least strikingly similar symptoms. Such revelations are sometimes accompanied by the explanation that "no one talked about those things in those days."

Wanting to talk to others can be an important first step toward breaking down feelings of isolation and impoverished self-image and providing an opportunity to affirm one's competence by helping others as well as receiving help (Schild and Black, 1984). Marsha Saxton describes the powerful benefits of one-to-one sharing: "I have learned about the necessity of having a peer, someone whose own personal knowledge of what I was sharing would reduce my fear of self-disclosure and allow me to really tell. . . . I have learned that a peer does not have to be someone with the same or even a very similar type of disability. . . . I remember, for example, being intrigued by a special connection I felt with a woman who had a cleft lip. When we met, we discovered a common theme in our self-images: a sense of not having been welcomed into the world (due, we guessed, to the reactions of our parents and others at the time of our birth to the would-be-perfect babies)."

THE BENEFITS AND LIMITATIONS OF SUPPORT GROUPS

Some people never go further than talking to another person and sharing experiences. For others, one-to-one encounters are a stimulus to involvement with a group, and for them group activities can be the key to empowerment. The mother of a child with Miller syndrome, an extremely rare genetic condition involving severe facial and limb anomalies, started a genetic support group soon after meeting just one other parent of a child like hers: "That isolated feeling left and I was filled with hope. I knew then that I had to do the same for others by being there to help them. I wonder if that philosophy came from all my years in Catholic school?"

A sense of affinity begins to take place along with affiliation with a support group. Regardless of the level of involvement, be it attending a meeting to hear a speaker or to find some comfortable kind of social activity or merely reading a quarterly newsletter, an individual begins to open up to the many possibilities offered by an organized group.

Support groups empower members to speak out. (National Down Syndrome Society)

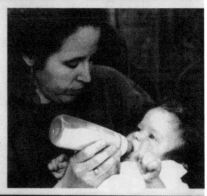

RECIPE DU JOUR

How can we give our kids who are still able to swallow the amount of fluid, protein and calories they need to grow and flourish? Lee read the ingredients of PediSure and came up with her own concoction, which I would venture to say other parents came up with as well. She mixes blended fruits (strawberries, raspberries, mangos, bananas, etc.) and powered milk into instant breakfasts. Zeva gets about 20 ounces plus a day, plus around 700 calories and a fair amount of protein. She loses a few ounces to seizures and projectile vomiting. Very often we see a seizure coming (Zeva turns pale, unstable and essentially out of it before she vomits) and we try to actually startle her to get her out of a trance. Usually it works, but occasionally we startle her more and wind up cleaning rancid instant breakfast tailings off ourselves. The recipe might work with children using G-tubes, as well.

Recycled Paper ♻

Parents share techniques as well as coping strategies. The National Tay-Sachs and Allied Diseases Association (1994) collected this kind of practical information and published a book with applications across disabilities: The Home Care Book: A Parent's Guide to Caring for Children with Progressive Neurological Diseases.

Making that first connection, whether by phone, in person, or through a newsletter, can change despair into hope and begin the healing of a person's fractured sense of self-worth. A young man with Klinefelter syndrome wrote the following to the founder of his genetic support group:

> Few people really make an impact on society, even less use their ability to serve misunderstood people, to be their voice. What you and your staff have done for me, helping me to understand my past, myself, and to show me that all my trouble in school, not to mention all the psychiatrists I had to see back then wasn't because I was simply crazy or mental (which by age 16 my family believed, they put me in a nut house for 13 months at age 15). You've shown me that all the hell I endured all my life wasn't my fault, but . . . what they did to me is almost unforgivable. I'm now 31, a 47, XXY. Diagnosed at age 27. . . . You've shown me that I'm normal and capable of being an everyday American citizen.

Many newly diagnosed families are unfamiliar with the concept of a support group. When told about a group concerned with their genetic condition, they are fearful that within a genetic support group they will meet others who have the same genetic disorder but with many more severe symptoms. Even if they themselves are severely affected by the genetic disorder, they may not wish a face-to-face encounter with reality (Weiss, 1989). On the other hand, they may be fearful of losing control of their emotions or of having to take on the burden of other people's problems. They may worry about being unable to reach out to others when they are so absorbed in their own suffering. At the other end of the spectrum are those who may envision the group as being a panacea, offering a magic potion that will heal their wounds.

Newcomers must be prepared for a sharing experience that includes more information than they may be ready to hear. Some parents may not wish to hear about children who are worse than theirs; other parents may not be equipped to handle the fact that some children are less affected than their own. Varying expectations underscore the need for a skillful group facilitator—a professional or trained participant. A facilitator with a certain degree of detachment is important to make the group experience valuable for all participants, regardless of where they are in the coping process.

Some individuals join support groups with unconscious motives, such as a need to escape a home situation involving the person with the genetic disorder. If these people become group leaders, they tend to throw themselves completely into organizational activities and networking with other local and national groups. It is not unusual for their lives outside of the group to become chaotic, with disruption in the home and on the job. Eventually, either they are forced out of the group or they force the group to dissolve.

Other precautions should be kept in mind (Bennett, 1990):

- Publications, group sessions, and fund-raising articles sometimes dwell upon worst-case scenarios. For individuals or families with a recent diagnosis, such horror stories can be frightening as well as off-putting.

- Groups that cover several distinct but related disorders may generalize and fail to differentiate among the needs of people affected by the different conditions as well as by different expressions of symptoms within a single disorder. For example, some persons with Gaucher disease show no symptoms, while others have severe blood and bone complications.

- While in theory a group should not be judgmental, in reality groups do sometimes reflect the attitudes held by the majority. Consequently, new members of a well-established group must face the possibility that they may not always receive the approval they seek. For example, the group may not support a couple's decision to terminate a pregnancy or one person's decision to separate from a spouse whom he or she holds responsible for their child's genetic disorder.

- Conflicts can arise if the attitudes of the majority of a group are shaped by shared cultural, religious, or ethnic background. At the very least, those from different backgrounds may feel isolated and may not find the support they expect. Some people may find comfort in the religious themes embraced by many groups, while others may not. People who believe that illness is a punishment for sinning or the result of a curse or someone's casting an "evil eye" may grapple with issues that never arise for a person who views genetic conditions within a strictly scientific context.

- Some individuals seek support from a group while still in crisis. They may bring with them many conflicting emotions, which the group is expected to help resolve. Groups are not always prepared for assessing when a member needs a different kind of help. The help offered by a genetic support group cannot substitute for professional attention when it is needed. When feelings of sadness persist too long, for example, a person might be suffering from depression and should seek professional help. Group members are not usually trained as psychotherapists or as genetic counselors. Even if they are, they should not function as such within their own group unless they have identified their role as professional.

It is well to remember the limitations of genetic support groups:

- The group cannot heal all personal wounds.
- Some groups go out of existence once the original need is met.
- Genetic support groups cannot substitute for professional help.
- Not all genetic patients are candidates for support groups.
- During family crises, a counselor is sometimes preferable.
- The timing of the referral to a group is critical.

There are times when members of a group need more than the group can give them, even when they have been involved for years. A referral to a therapist for individual, couple, or family therapy might be indicated during a family crisis, around the anniversary of the death of a genetically affected child, when a marriage is threatened, or before hospitalization. However, members may well return to the support group when the crisis is over and they have obtained appropriate professional help.

Members should continue to seek referrals to qualified health care professionals as changing physical, social, and emotional needs require, and these referrals should be handled in an orderly, consistent way. The timing of referral, the identification of professional resources, the designation of who makes the referral, and the establishment of the support group's referral network are all critical (Weigle, 1986). Social workers, genetic counselors, or nurses who serve as consultants or advisors to the group can make appropriate referrals and can also help with the development of a referral list (Black and Weiss, 1990).

— 3 —

Peer Support

Peer support involves a one-to-one relationship between two individuals who are at different points on a continuum of shared experience. The peer supporter is someone who has been through a crisis similar to that of the one receiving the support and who has dealt with it constructively. Consequently, the helper is a veteran who may be able to provide unique emotional and informational support from "having been there" (Santelli, 1990).

To act as a peer support helper, a person must have worked out his or her own problems. The helper must be willing to keep all information in the strictest confidence as well as refrain from giving advice (Poyadue, 1990). Peer support does not replace professional help. Trained peer helpers need to have a clear idea of their role in providing support to individuals and families and not attempt to provide psychotherapy or take the place of a physician. The peer supporter should know that, even for individuals affected by the same genetic condition, everyone's medical needs are unique. "The peer helper must recognize that he or she cannot change a family diagnosis or eliminate their grief. The helper cannot provide daily support to a family. They cannot solve financial problems, provide child care or transportation. The peer helper should not allow a family to drain them so that they can no longer listen, empathize and care. The peer helper should not feel guilty or inadequate if a family cannot adjust to having a member with special needs or if their offer of help is rejected" (Trombino and Bernhardt, 1990).

There are many models for providing peer support but the most effective are complete programs that have a systematic approach of matching trained helpers with new people who have been referred to the program. Key to the matching is having a large enough pool of experienced helpers that the needs of people with diverse backgrounds and ideas can be met. To facilitate meaningful encounters, volunteer helpers should be trained in effective communication and empathetic listening as well as in strategies for providing resources and information. Depending on the situation, a match may require a single exchange or follow-up contacts over an extended period of time. Contacts may be in person or by telephone. An appropriate system of record keeping must be maintained. The program itself and its component parts, especially training, matching, and follow-up, must have an evaluation component. The Association for Children with Down Syndrome, Inc., is an example of an organization that has a parent peer counselor training program that prepares parents to provide supportive counseling interventions. All of these peer helpers work under social work supervision and are matched by the social workers after a screening process has taken place. The confidentiality of peer counseling contacts is protected within the parameters of the social worker / peer counselor / parent relationship (Smith, 1990).

Although peer support programs tend to involve the parents of children with genetic or other disabilities, other family members, including affected individuals, can participate as well. A program linking patients with a recent diagnosis of chronic renal disease such as polycystic kidney disease to trained peer volunteers, for example, follows a traditional format (Calder, 1990, p. 9):

> The patient is asked if he or she wishes to speak with a People to People volunteer. If so, the patient completes a consent form, and the volunteer or professional calls the People to People coordinator. The coordinator matches that patient with a peer volunteer. Matching is based on as many common variables as possible, i.e., age, sex, marital status, number of children, current, anticipated, and past treatment modalities, and location. The peer volunteer is requested to meet face to face with the referred patient within 5 days of the referral. Evaluation forms are sent to both the peer volunteer and the new patient 6 weeks after the referral to assess the match and the services.

At a national conference on peer support training held by the Alliance of Genetic Support Groups in 1990, keynote speaker Judith Tindall listed considerations that are necessary before setting up a peer helping program:

1. Decide on the needs of your particular group.
2. Decide on the rationale.
3. Decide on the goals of your training and your target population.
4. Develop a selection procedure.
5. Adopt a curriculum for basic training and advance training for the population.
6. Devise a system of supervision.
7. Develop a system in which the activities can be accomplished.
8. Develop a proposed budget and a means for funding.
9. Develop a plan for gaining support staff and outreach to the community.
10. Come up with facilities.
11. Decide on a means of evaluation, including program evaluation, training evaluation, and evaluation of outcomes.

Groups that do not have a central office, staff, or a single telephone contact need to set up a system for handling first-time callers. An experienced peer helper advises: "When the phone rings, and it is a first contact, the volunteer needs to leave behind the personal world, and turn on that listening ear. In an instant, one needs to be empathetic, sympathetic, diplomatic and realistic. It does help to have a 3" by 5" card with not only key words, but the steps to be taken . . . and paper for easy access to names and addresses of knowledgeable health professionals" (Stickney, 1990).

Little People of America's Bay Area (California) chapter receives most of its first contacts over the phone. They recommend a number of practical procedures:

1. Get statistics: the name and birth date of the affected person, names of parents, names and ages of siblings, complete address, and phone number.
2. Find out what professional health care the family has had; if needed, offer potential referrals in their locale.

3. Describe the items that will be sent in an informational packet.

4. If the family is ready, arrange for a personal visit from someone with a similar situation who has had training and experience in making a first visit.

5. Although one individual can serve as a "buddy," the new family should be encouraged to attend group gatherings, but they should not be suffocated by overzealous attention.

There are times when an individual or family who has just received a genetic diagnosis does not want to get involved with a genetic support group but is eager to talk with someone about the impact of the diagnosis. For these people, it is critical that health care providers know about peer support programs and be willing to refer to them. It is up to the professional and peer helpers to assure families that, if they want to contact the group, they can do so at a later time.

— 4 —

How to Organize a Genetic Support Group

I'm doing what I have to do, what I'm driven to do.

SUSAN FETTES, founder
Beckwith-Wiedemann Support Network

There is no formula for starting a genetic support group that guarantees successful results. Yet, as with raising a child, definite milestones mark the evolution of a group that starts at one individual's kitchen table and becomes a structured legal entity that qualifies as a voluntary health group. These developmental stages are not pegged to a timetable, however; nor is their achievement a reliable precursor of a long or healthy organizational life. Rather, each stage reflects the individuals involved at the time, and if we were keeping a growth chart, it would be more useful for measuring the development of the parents than the child. Nevertheless, there are some key steps to take in developing a support group:

1. Organize around a specific issue.
2. Clarify the purpose of the organization.
3. Select your strategies carefully.
4. Avoid detailed planning and capitalize on opportunities.
5. Get started by figuring out what has to be done.
6. Let leaders emerge from the group.

7. Find a role for everyone who wants to help.

8. Identify what each person does best.

9. Concentrate on whether the organization is achieving its goals.

10. Make sure members feel that their work is appreciated.

Keep in mind the difference between a support group, which is a loosely defined group of people sharing common experiences and difficulties, and a voluntary health group, which is a nonprofit, member-supported, viable financial entity with goals that encompass education, advocacy, and research (Ciccariello, 1993). Genetic support groups are frequently both. Not all genetic support groups have a self-help component, even though mutual aid or self-help may be a by-product of the work of the organization. The terms *self-help* and *mutual aid* are interchangeable, but *support* has a wider, more general connotation. Support can be offered to group members in a variety of ways: by empathy and understanding from others in the group who have "been there" in the coping process; by financial aid for medical equipment; by working to improve the laws protecting the rights of people with disabilities; or by educating the public about a genetic disorder.

Perhaps the most meaningful advice to be given about starting a group is to recognize from the outset that nothing works for everyone in the same way forever. In many ways, groups have a life of their own. They grow and change along with the people who make up the group. The purpose of a group can expand or even change as new information is discovered. Or the needs and interests of the people involved may shift from those of the group's founders, necessitating the adoption of new goals and objectives. Most people don't start out to establish a group; rather, they are motivated to meet a highly personal need, such as overcoming an overwhelming sense of isolation, fear, frustration, or helplessness. As one mother said, "I was being very selfish, if the truth be known. I wanted to be comforted by others who must be experiencing what I was going through."

For some people, like Melissa, the founder of K. S. and Associates, the search for others was the first step toward starting a group. She and her pediatrician looked for an established support group for families with Klinefelter syndrome and came to the conclusion that there was none. What followed is the genesis of one genetic support group.

Melissa wrote to Ann Landers, asking her to help contact other families. At first, the famous newspaper columnist agreed to print the letter. Then she declined because the syndrome was too rare and her editors had questioned Melissa's statistics that Klinefelter syndrome can affect as many as one in four hundred males. Finally, she agreed to publish the letter if the group had a post office box to receive any answers. Melissa chose the name K. S. and Associates because she needed a name on the postal application. She wanted to remain anonymous, and the name had a corporate ring to it that she liked.

On April 12, 1989, the letter was printed. On April 13 there were 13 letters in the P.O. box. On April 14 there were 30 letters. On April 15 there were 40 letters. On April 30 there were 134 letters. By the end of the summer, a thousand letters had been received. Melissa answered each letter personally, at first, then with a form letter and a short note. Along with the letters came unsolicited donations. After she had $900 in checks made out to K. S. and Associates, Melissa realized that she had an organization with a name, an address, and a soon-to-be-established checking account. She had people with shared concerns and a growing list of things to do.

Without any real forethought, Melissa had founded a genetic support group. She recalls that it was completely unplanned in the beginning. Quickly, she came to appreciate that she had started something by asking, is anybody else out there? Having raised expectations, she took it upon herself to take further action. As more families shared their stories, patterns of behavior and personal successes of men with Klinefelter syndrome emerged that differed greatly from what the medical community was telling patients to expect. The cases were not nearly as devastating as the literature described, but the emotional problems experienced by the families were not being acknowledged or addressed by health care providers. The needs of the people sharing with each other helped shape the group and determine its purpose.

Within a few years, K. S. and Associates evolved into an educational, nonprofit organization dedicated to increasing public awareness of Klinefelter syndrome (and other male sex chromosome variations) and providing support and information to those dealing with the syndrome. Melissa has become the executive director. The organization publishes a newsletter called the *Even Exchange* and sponsors regional support group meetings and a national conference.

As is clear from Melissa's story, founders don't always carefully plot out the trip before they set out. There are organizations, books, and resources that make the journey easier, but most people stumble upon them along the way. If and when they have time to read about the process they have been living, they discover helpful hints that elicit an impatient "Where was this when I needed it?" It can be equally frustrating to discover after the fact the existence of organizations such as the Alliance of Genetic Support Groups, the National Organization for Rare Disorders, and the American Self-Help Clearinghouse that have resources and expertise to help new groups get off on the right foot.

---

1. Check resource directories and national organizations.
2. Identify existing groups with similar concerns.
3. Write a simple announcement.
4. Share information with everyone you know.
5. Contact geneticists, genetic counselors, and other providers.
6. Identify state and regional genetics coordinators.
7. Ask a reference librarian to help locate resource directories.
8. Write a letter to *Exceptional Parent* magazine.
9. Inform radio and television producers.
10. Network to get the word out about the group.

It comes down to individual style. Some people are researchers: they have a nose for networks and ask everyone for help. Others plunge right in and figure out what to do as they go along. Be aware that developing an organization is a job in itself, and how it is done can help or hinder the actual work of the group.

FINDING OTHERS

The first step is to check national resource directories to see if any similar organizations already exist. National groups such as the Alli-

NEW SUPPORT GROUP FOR NAGER AND MILLER SYNDROMES

Recently, I, along with Margaret Ieronimo, started The Foundation for Nager and Miller Syndromes. My seven-year-old daughter, Melissa, has Nager syndrome; Margaret's two-year-old daughter, Bridget, has Miller syndrome.

These very rare syndromes create maxillocraniofacial anomalies as well as various degrees of limb deformities. Many of these children end up having tracheostomies and gastrostomies. Extensive plastic surgery is required (or at times create) ears, lower jaws, eyes, and more, depending on each case.

Our foundation will serve as a support network for families affected by these syndromes. We will have a free newsletter. We will also conduct outreach to the medical community.

Families are invited to become a part of our foundation. For more information, write to: **The Foundation for Nager and Miller Syndromes,** 721 S. Carlisle, South Bend, Ind. 46619, or call (219) 289-5611 (for parents with children who have Nager syndrome) or (708) 729-0701 (for parents with children who have Miller syndrome).

Pam LeBaron
Indiana

Letters to the editor can reach families who need to know about your group. (Reprinted with the expressed consent and approval of Exceptional Parent*)*

ance of Genetic Support Groups, the National Organization for Rare Disorders, and the American Self-Help Clearinghouse can provide much of this information. If no group exists, they may have information about families or professionals with an interest in the disorder who are willing to be contacted.

If there is a group with the same or similar concerns, find out what they do and how they do it. It is worth investigating known groups before undertaking the extensive outreach necessary to find others who have the same unmet needs and concerns. It might be just as effective to join forces by establishing a local chapter or supporting that group's mission as it would be to start a new group.

Once you determine that a new group is needed, it can be launched with a simple announcement that includes information about the proposed group, the genetic disorder of primary concern, and a contact person's name, address, and telephone number. At this point, there is no need to be too specific. For new groups organizing around rare disorders, however, it helps to describe the disorder in some detail in any public statement, because most people, professional and consumer, will probably not have heard of it.

This announcement should be disseminated widely, with a special effort to reach geneticists, genetic counselors, and other health care providers such as physicians, nurses, and medical social workers. The Alliance of Genetic Support Groups can provide the name of each state genetics coordinator and regional maternal and child health directors, who should all be interested in learning about a potential new group. A list of the ten regional genetics networks is found in Appendix B.

Major genetics centers can help identify professionals who have an interest in the specific disorder. These individuals can be primary resources for connecting families. Respecting confidentiality, they won't give out the names of people they treat; however, they can play an invaluable role by informing their patients about the potential for a new group and by offering to link families and organizers.

A reference librarian at the local public library can easily locate directories useful for building a resource list and eventually a mailing list (Ciccariello, 1986). Useful texts include the *American Hospital Association Directory*, which lists hospitals with specialties, and the *AAMC Directory of American Medical Education*, which lists medical schools, clinical facilities, and names of the heads of medical departments. Membership directories of the American Society of Human Genetics, the American College of Medical Genetics, and the National Society of Genetic Counselors, which include geographical listings of their members, may also contain relevant information.

Most organizations have newsletters. They will usually print an announcement about the formation of a new genetic support group. People discover an amazing amount of information by reading letters to the editor. This popular form of free publicity should not be overlooked. *Exceptional Parent* magazine runs a listing of new groups, as do the newsletters published by each of the regional genetics networks (see Appendix B). A letter to radio and television producers is less likely to get results, but since they are always in need of human interest stories, it does not hurt to send information. The key to success at this early stage is network, network, network. Use any and every opportunity to get the word out.

ASSESSING NEEDS

Once potential members for a group have been identified, it is necessary to find out whether they are interested in joining a support group and, if so, what type of group they wish to have. The Alliance of Genetic Support Groups developed a needs-assessment survey to help new groups identify initial goals and objectives. This survey can help identify where the most interest is: peer support, research, education, legislation, advocacy, networking, or who knows what. Prospective members may want a group to embrace all of these goals or just a few. Regardless, it will be necessary to set priorities and to keep in mind that these will surely change as the organization begins to function and grow.

A good deal of thought should be given to what kind of group is needed. Whom will it serve—individuals affected by a definite genetic diagnosis? Or family members, such as spouses, siblings, and grandparents? Will health care providers, such as genetic counselors, geneticists, nurses, and social workers, be welcome? Can anyone, consumer or professional, participate?

In addition to making decisions about the composition of the group, what is its purpose? It is not possible to anticipate every need in the beginning, nor will it be possible to meet every need at any one time. Often a group forms to fulfill one particular function, and as it grows, it takes on other tasks to fill gaps identified by its members. The Huntington's Disease Society of America, for example, began as an advocacy group and now has many other services, such as support group meetings for families, a handbook for caregivers, and training sessions for social workers.

Sometimes, groups change the structure of their organization to meet the specific needs of some members. In a meeting of an ongoing support group representing neurofibromatosis, the discussion leader observed that certain young, unmarried women seemed to feel inhibited about asking personal questions. Not obviously affected by the disorder, they had emerging concerns about dating and sexuality. They found it difficult to raise their concerns in the presence of the severely affected, older members. They did not identify with them, yet they feared that they might develop the same symptoms of the disease. The group leaders concluded that a separate group would be more beneficial for individuals like these mildly affected women, and the original group was reconstituted to serve the older, more seriously affected members (Schild and Black, 1984).

One of the best ways to start a group is to find models to follow. Betsy Wilson, a member of five different support groups and the leader of Let's Face It, tells new organizers to get a card file. She advises writing all new information on cards and filing it under titles like "patients," "families," "doctors," "TV folks," or "nurses." The

Needs Assessment Survey for Genetic Support Groups

- Are you a parent of a child with a genetic disorder? _____.
- Are you a grandparent of a child with a genetic disorder? _____.
- Are you a sibling of someone with a genetic disorder? _____.
- Are you a spouse of someone with a genetic disorder? _____.
- Do you yourself have a genetic disorder? _____.
- Are you at risk for inheriting a genetic disorder? _____.
- Are you a friend of someone with a genetic disorder? _____.
- Are you interested in the support group as a health care professional? _____.
- How did you find out about this support group?
  By newsletter _____.
  From an acquaintance _____, physician _____, genetic counselor _____, nurse _____, social worker _____, other professional _____.
  From a family member _____.
  From a listing in a journal or other media _____.
  Other _____.
- What do you hope to receive from your genetic support group?
  Support _____.
  A way to give back _____.
  Sympathy _____.
  Information about treatment _____.
  Medical advice _____.
  Information about research _____.
  Technical advice _____.
  Advice on coping skills _____.
  Information about resources _____.
  Other _____. Please describe _____.
- Which organizational activities would be most important to you? (Check all that interest you.)
  Support group discussion meetings _____.
  Educational lectures on the genetic disorder _____.
  Workshops on various subjects _____.
  Fund-raising activities to promote research _____.
  Advocacy activities _____.
  Networking with other genetic support groups _____.
  Social activities _____.
  Newsletters _____.
  Other _____. Please describe _____.

- If you want group meetings, how often would you be willing to attend?
  Monthly _____.
  Quarterly _____.
  Yearly _____.
- Would you be willing to travel more than one hour? _____.
- Is transportation a problem for you? _____.
- Would you come by yourself? _____.
  With a family member? _____.
  With a friend? _____.
- Can you volunteer time for group activities or planning committees? _____.
- Would you like to communicate with other group members on a one-to-one basis? _____.
  (This kind of help is known as *peer support.* Peer support implies a one-to-one relationship between two people that involves sharing information, ideas, experiences, offering support and validating emotional responses.)
- Would you be interested in receiving peer support?
  Yes _____.
  No _____.
  Not certain _____.
- If so, in person? _____.
  By telephone? _____.
  By letter? _____.
- Would you be interested in being trained to give peer support?
  Yes _____.
  No _____.
  Not certain _____.
- Would you want the group to offer a peer support program?
  Yes _____.
  No _____.
  Not certain _____.
- Additional comments or recommendations for group activities: _____.

next step is to go to leaders of organizations similar to the one desired and ask them for advice. They can provide the name of local accountants, lawyers, and others familiar with the needs of nonprofit organizations. There is plenty of free help available. Ask!

Mary Ann Wilson recalls her start:

In 1979, I was watching a local television program featuring area geneticists who said that the most effective way to get out the information about any genetic condition was to get organized. A grandmother was able to get her question about neurofibromatosis on the air, and I called the station to get her number. We then started a local group after learning from a pediatric neurologist that a national group has just been established. We learned that a physician at the National Institutes of Health was on the advisory board of the national organization and was interested in NF. As it turned out, he was a proponent of voluntary organizations and encouraged us to establish a local group for NF families.

Since our family has stable finances and my children with no medical problems were in school, I took on the role of organizer. My being voted The Best All Around in high school was perhaps somewhat prophetic because the organizer has to do everything at the beginning.

Jodi Zwain took a different course. After the birth and eventual diagnosis of her son with Russell-Silver syndrome, said to affect only two hundred people in the United States, she decided to search for other families. She obtained a list of seventeen names from the National Organization for Rare Disorders and wrote to each one. She described her family's experiences and asked for a response so she could compile the information into a newsletter for sharing information and advice. Her mother made the first donation for stationery. Her father served as the group's lawyer, and his accountant was recruited for financial services. The informal network has grown into an incorporated not-for-profit association, with members in the United States, Italy, Canada, and Australia. It has a board of directors, professional advisors, a brochure, regional liaisons, a quarterly newsletter, and a growing fund-raising base.

ORGANIZATIONAL LEADERSHIP

In the beginning I felt driven to organize the group. *Passion* may be a better word for what I felt. Organizing the group was great for me personally: it gave my life a very positive focus. It was very therapeutic to have my mind on the group and other families instead of thinking about how unfair it was that my daughter was born with a rare genetic condition. This is not just a job—this is my life.

MARIANNE HAVEN, founder
Pallister-Killian Family Support Group

Groups start with dreams, and no one expects them to be replaced with nightmares. However, with success can come tremendous demands from different directions. Members' personal needs can sometimes be in conflict with the needs of the growing organization. Group plans can easily be diverted by unexpected family problems that take precedence. Change can trigger chaos. The lack of change can result in stagnation. So much depends on the quality and skills of the group's leaders.

Various criteria can be applied to evaluate a person's potential to be a successful group leader:

- Desire to be a helper
- Time to give to the group
- Willingness to phase out
- Skills in monitoring changing needs of the group
- Communication skills and the ability to listen
- Knowledge of the genetic disorder the group represents
- Awareness of community resources
- Ability to be nonjudgmental

The publication *Sickle Cell Mutual Help Groups* lists similar criteria for effective group leaders:

- The person must want to be a helper.
- The leader must allot enough time to take on responsibilities and give needed attention to group concerns.
- Groups are dynamic; leaders need to value and understand the nature of personal change.
- Leaders must be willing to phase themselves out over time and become resource persons, allowing leadership to arise from within the group. Groups can help this process by giving individual members specific tasks or responsibilities that will help them develop their own skills.

- Leaders must constantly monitor group needs and adjust the group, the content of meetings, and leadership roles as membership needs change and dictate.

Genetic self-help or mutual aid groups are usually led by a member or peer facilitator. Voluntary genetic organizations that have a broader focus can be led by either a consumer or a professional or sometimes, by a combination of the two. Even when an organization has a paid staff, however, highly involved lay leaders are necessary. Voluntary health groups are the training ground for individuals who frequently cross that fine line between consumers and professionals. Many professional volunteers, in fact, have come from the world of health voluntaries.

Abbey Meyers, president of NORD, believes that the key to leadership lies in the difference between the person who is angry with or accepts fate and the person who says, "I can't sit around and wait for someone to find a cure, I have to go out there and do something about it." But once "out there," Abbey predicts, self-motivated activists will find complications and unexpected challenges that compound their original problem. They naturally seek out other families affected by the same condition as an obvious source of help and advice and, eventually, form a group for the mutual support that comes from talking to each other. Abbey suggests that "leaders emerge from these groups when they no longer have the need to talk, and when they learn how to listen."

While it is rare to have the luxury of seeking a leader as opposed to becoming one by default because no one else has volunteered, certain qualities and skills are reliable indicators of a person's leadership potential. *You Are Not Alone: A Guide to Establishing Huntington's Disease Support Groups* (Greene, 1992) lists some of these:

- Group skills
- Communication skills
- Knowledge of the genetic disorder in question
- Awareness of community resources

- Empathy
- Ability to be nonjudgmental

Experienced organizers recommend that a professional and an experienced lay leader colead a new group until consumer leaders develop necessary group and communication skills. It is particularly important in self-help groups, where peer support is the essential ingredient in the group's operations, that leaders be consumers. In all groups, however, it is up to responsible, responsive lay leaders to call upon professionals when necessary to ensure that the group functions for the benefit of all involved.

BEWARE OF BURNOUT

A healthy group nurtures and trains new leaders. The knowledge that others share the responsibility for building the program and the workload will help prevent volunteer burnout, a condition often fatal to small groups that depend heavily on a few active volunteers. Burnout has psychological, emotional, and physical manifestations. It strikes individuals who have used up all of their resources and have nothing left to give. For them, what was once a dream has become a nightmare. Everything seems to be an overwhelming effort.

Some of the people who suffer from this real affliction feel victimized. They believe that no one recognizes their contributions or values their many personal sacrifices. The good feelings that energized them when they began as enthusiastic new volunteers are gone and are replaced by anger, disappointment, and incredible fatigue.

One woman who had served as the president of her group for seven years dropped out and wouldn't even give a donation during the annual fund drive. Looking back, she realized that she had taken on all the responsibilities herself until she just "could not do it anymore." Never comfortable saying no, she had to cut all ties to the group to which she had dedicated years of selfless service in order to say yes to her own needs.

Burned-out volunteers lack balance. Although most of the time it is true that it is better to give than receive, many people who start groups are so focused on others' unmet needs that they fail to notice when their own needs are not being met. The founder of a genetic support group with members scattered around the world recalled: "I dreamed that I was on an operating table. Both arms were attached to long plastic tubes. I knew I needed a blood transfusion, but as I got weaker and weaker, I realized all the blood was being drained out and none was being pumped back in." When she quit, the organization was on the verge of bankruptcy, the executive director was being sued by one of the chapters, and national board meetings were battlegrounds. She could not make the group functional by herself. Ultimately, people with different ways of operating picked up the pieces and began again.

Sometimes, the problem is not a lack of volunteers or committed workers. Rather, it is an inability or unwillingness on the part of the founder to let go. "Founder flounder" is a common condition, and it can seriously delay or prevent a group's development. Despite the best intentions of the founder, the group remains a passion or pet project and never evolves into a cohesive group that can sustain itself. It can be painful, even destructive, when the needs of the members conflict with those of the person or people who started the group. At such potentially explosive junctures, it is critical to establish an open process for resolving differences. It is to be hoped that members show feelings of mutual respect and share a vision of what they all want their group to be. Without trust in one another and a belief that the group serves a larger purpose, the process won't work. Perhaps most important is the recognition that change is a constant. Change is inevitable and should be welcomed as a positive source of vital energy.

Difficulties arise when leaders begin to believe that there is only one way to do things or only one thing to be done. Reasons for starting a group become subsumed by rationales for maintaining the status quo. More time is spent giving advice than sharing information. Complaints about what is wrong drain volunteers of energy needed to make things better. There is too much to do and too much to know. What is simple becomes complex; what is straightforward becomes confusing. The idea of change causes anxiety and sparks feelings of powerlessness and isolation. The conditions are strikingly similar to those that gave rise to the group in the first place. No wonder people drop out or back away, particularly when they have serious personal problems.

Attitude plays a major role in burnout. Everyone has days when mailing a letter or making a bank deposit can cause instant overload. More time is spent worrying about what has to be done than actually doing anything. Consequently, it becomes harder and harder to complete routine tasks, much less undertake long-term projects. There is no time to do what needs to be done and less time for planning what to do next. Certainly no time can be found to evaluate what's been done to determine whether it is worth doing again. Furthermore, there is a certain comfort in routine. The results may not be up to expectation, but who is willing to risk changing? Only those people who don't do anything. The people calling for change aren't the ones who raise the money, do the work, run the group. They take the work of the group for granted. They sometimes expect even more. They don't appreciate all that is being done for them. Some don't take advice. Others don't agree with group positions on social issues such as adoption or abortion, medical procedures like bone marrow transplants, or programmatic priorities.

Feelings of discontent can escalate into personal hostility. Leaders frequently resent the efforts of others calling for change, seeing them as a challenge to individual control. The result is eventually fight or flight: the group is fractured by dissention, or the leader leaves.

There is a way to protect both leaders and the group, and it starts with attitudinal adjustment. For people who try too hard, it only gets harder. Think about hurrying: When we try to walk fast, we actually slow up; muscles tighten, impeding progress. But when we relax, we move along at a much quicker pace. A positive attitude releases the brakes that slow us down. It expands time so that there is always enough. It quiets the nagging internal voice that generates feelings of guilt: You haven't done enough; If you really cared, you would [fill in the blank].

Further, a positive attitude opens us to the possibilities of life. It frees us to take risks by taking the sting out of failure. There is real power in having enough faith in oneself to allow ourselves to fail. By extension, we exhibit faith in others by allowing them to think for themselves and to make their own decisions. By giving others time, attention, and respect, we facilitate a true group process that benefits all.

THE PARTNERSHIP BETWEEN CONSUMERS AND PROFESSIONALS

May I know my knowledge and its limits.
May I learn what you know.
May you learn what I know.
Together may we learn to do what is best.

Y. E. HSIA
"To Strive for the Best, Together"

Consumers and professionals working together represent the best chance for getting a group off to a strong start. Professionals have access to information, resources, and potential members. Consumers have the passion and drive that are essential ingredients in starting a group. As a result of the depersonalization of health care, however, families don't always have opportunities to work closely with genetic counselors or social workers and may be wary of too much, or even any, professional involvement in a new group. Some professionals, on the other hand, are fearful of patient autonomy and do not support efforts that enable patients and families to take care of themselves and others. When trust and mutual respect are nurtured, however, the result is usually a healthy, productive relationship, where everyone involved benefits.

When families and professionals collaborate, certain goals can be set (see Bishop, Woll, and Arango, 1993):

- Promote a relationship in which family members and professionals work together to ensure the best services for the child and the family.

- Recognize and respect the knowledge, skills, and experience that families and professionals bring to the relationship.

- Acknowledge that the development of trust is an integral part of a collaborative relationship.

- Facilitate open communication so that families and professionals feel free to express themselves.

- Create an atmosphere in which the cultural traditions, values, and diversity of families are acknowledged and honored.

- Recognize that negotiation is essential in a collaborative relationship.

- Bring to the relationship the mutual commitment of families, professionals, and communities to meet the needs of children with special needs and their families.

Groups can be an extension of the health care that providers offer their patients and, therefore, are considered by many to be an important component of the health care team. Professionals, whether in genetic counseling, pediatrics, obstetrics, nursing, or social work, are in an excellent position to evaluate a patient's need for a group. They recognize that not all parents or children are good candidates for genetic support groups. Many do better by seeking help within

Conferences provide a forum where professionals and families can work together. (National Marfan Foundation)

their family network or by working with a therapist on a one-to-one basis. Some children may do best in a cross-disability or age-related support group in a hospital or clinic setting.

Timing is also a critical factor. Many individuals and families need time to react to a genetic diagnosis before braving a meeting with complete strangers. That initial contact, whether face to face or on the telephone, can represent a parent or patient's first encounter with reality. Anticipatory guidance by the referring professional who is familiar with the group and its members can increase the chances of a successful experience. Sometimes professionals find it useful just to write the name of the group and contact information on a card and hand it to the patient for when, if ever, he or she feels ready to reach out.

If no group exists for people with a particular disorder, a professional can help develop it, guide it until potential leadership is developed among the core group of consumers, and offer ongoing assistance as required or requested. According to Ed Madara of the American Self-Help Clearinghouse (1990), "Some groups refer to this ideal professional role as being 'on tap, not on top.' " The shape of this help should be determined by the group members.

Professionals can link groups to local, state, and national resources. They can direct members' attention to legislation that may have an impact on the access to existing genetic services. They can train group members to gain access to public health and political arenas for their own and their families' benefit (Weiss, 1993). They can also help genetic support groups work toward eliminating discriminatory practices and policies that might affect their members in the areas of insurance, employment, education, and adoption. They can help members understand the issues of informed consent and confidentiality in genetic research. They can raise group consciousness about cultural differences, particularly when different attitudes about health and illness are relevant to outreach efforts and service programs.

In other words, professionals need to be flexible. They should offer to assist when professional involvement is required and help lay leaders to recognize situations that call for professional intervention. In all other instances, roles should be negotiated, and there need be no limits set on the contributions that anyone, professional or consumer, can make.

TEXAS GENETICS NETWORK

Texas Fiesta Educativa-TexGene '94

Collaboration: Linking Families to Education and Science
Colaboración: Uniendo Familias a La Educación y la Ciencia

26 y 27 de Agosto 1994   August 26 & 27, 1994

ST. ANTHONY HOTEL
SAN ANTONIO, TEXAS

La 6ª Conferencia Bilingüe
y Bicultural Estatal Para
Personas Con Impedimentos,
Sus Familias, Defensores,
y Profesionales

The 6ª Annual Bilingual/
Bicultural Statewide Conference
for Persons With Disabilities,
Families, Advocates, and
Professionals.

Patrocinado en parte por: **Funded in part by:**

Texas Planning Council for Developmental Disabilities
March of Dimes, Birth Defects Foundation
TexGene

August 24-25, 1994 — Texgene Committee Meetings

Texas Fiesta Educativa—TexGene '94

¿Quién Puede Participar?
Personas de habla español que tienen algun impedimento, que son padres o familiares de personas con impedimentos, además de profesionales, voluntarios o personas interesadas en proveer servicios a hispanos con impedimentos.

¿De Qué Se Trata?
* Una conferencia de dos días que ofrece una oportunidad para discutir una gran variedad de temas de importancia a hispanos con impedimentos y sus familias.
* La mayoría de las sesiones escogidas para el viernes serán en inglés pero también habrá sesiones en español que serán de interés a padres. La mayoría de las sesiones del sábado serán presentadas en español para ser de beneficio a personas hispanas con impedimentos y sus familias. Interpretes (Español o de Señas) serán disponibles.

El Precio de la Conferencia:
* EL PRECIO SI SE REGISTRA ANTES DE LA CONFERENCIA: $90.00 por persona o por familia para los dos días
* El PRECIO SI SE REGISTRA AL LLEGAR A LA CONFERENCIA: $100.00
* El Precio incluye materiales para la conferencia, 2 desayunos continentales, hora social el viernes, almuerzo el sábado, y guardería el sábado.

El Ultimo Día Para Registrase Con Anticipación:
22 de Julio de 1994. Haga sus chequees 2 nombre de: Texas Fiesta Educativa.

Para Reservar Habitación:
St. Anthony Hotel: 300 E. Travis St. Llame al 210-227-4392.
Precios: (mas impuestos) la noche por familia
    67.00 Sencillo   94.00 Triple or Cuádruple
    82.00 Doble
* Precio estatal a la disposición de personas que califica con identificación apropiada.

Guardería/Cuidado De Los Niños:
Este servicio es gratis y solo es ofrecido el sábado.
¡ESPACIO ES LIMITADO! Por favor indique su necesidad para este servicio de guardería en la Registración para la conferencia. Los primeros de pedir el servicio tendrán prioridad para recibir el servicio. Se ofrece este servicio solo a niños de 12 años o menor.

Asistencia Financiera:
Asistencia Financiera a su disposición para solicitantes que califican para cubrir parte de los gastos cuando se registra en la conferencia y gastos del hotel. Asistencia es limitada, por favor de llenar la Aplicación Financiera y la forma de Registracion para la Conferencia.

Para Más Información:
Si tiene algunas preguntas, comuníquese con Marvin Prevost
512-454-4816 1-800-223-4206.

Temas Incluirán:
Transición	Cómo obtener Servicios
Educación Especial	Defectos del Tubo Neural
Diagnosis Prenatal	Introdución a Gen'tica.

Who:
Spanish-speaking and Hispanic individuals with disabilities, parents and families of persons with disabilities, as well as the professionals, paraprofessionals and volunteers who serve Hispanic persons with disabilities.

What:
* A two-day conference offering comprehensive topics applicable to Spanish-speaking and Hispanic persons with disabilities and their family members.
* The workshops planned for Friday are geared toward professionals and will be conducted mostly in English. The Saturday workshops are geared towards Spanish-speaking individuals and will be conducted mostly in Spanish, although there will be some sessions available in English which professionals will find to be of interest. Sign language and Spanish/English interpreters will be available both days for the general sessions.

Registration Fee:
* PRE-REGISTRATION - $90.00 per individual/family for both days
* ON-SITE REGISTRATION - $100.00
* Registration includes Conference packet, 2 continental breakfasts, Friday social hour with entertainment, Saturday lunch, & Saturday child care.

Registration Deadline:
July 22, 1994. Make checks payable to Texas Fiesta Education.

Hotel Accommodations:
St. Anthony Hotel: 300 E. Travis St. Call 210-227-4392.
Room Rate: (plus taxes) per night (per family)
    67.00 Single   94.00 Triple or Quad
    82.00 double
* State rate available for qualified persons with proper identification.

Child Care:
Free child care will be provided on Saturday only, on a first come-first serve basis. SPACE IS LIMITED!, so please indicate your child care needs on the conference registration form. This service is only offered to children 12 years old and under.

Financial Assistance:
A limited number of stipends are available for qualified applicants to cover registration fees and hotel. Assistance is limited. Please complete Financial Aid/Scholarship Application and Conference Registration Form to apply.

Information:
If you have questions, please contact:
Marvin Prevost 512-454-4816 1-800-223-4206

Workshop Topics Will Include:
Transition: A Life-Long Process	How to Access Services
Special Education	Neural Tube Defects
Prenatal Diagnosis	Introduction to Genetics

The ten regional genetics networks bring together professionals and consumers for collaborative programing that addresses diverse needs. This bilingual conference announcement for the Texas Fiesta Educativa is a wonderful example of outreach that is sensitive to cultural differences. (Texas Genetics Network)

Principles that should rule the collaboration between families and professionals have been developed nationally by those specifically concerned with children with special health needs and their families. They offer important points of reference for any health-related group involving consumers and professionals.

1. Identify the need of the group.
2. Guide the group until consumer leadership develops.
3. Offer assistance (e.g., meeting rooms, referrals, getting speakers).
4. Serve on professional advisory board, if asked.
5. Serve as a clinical consultant.
6. Cofacilitate discussion groups.
7. Educate group members about new treatments.
8. Help evaluate research proposals.
9. Help with newsletter (e.g., write a column on medical issues).
10. Publicize the group.
11. Link the group to local, state, and national resources.
12. Help the group with advocacy strategies.
13. Help members understand genetic research projects.
14. Raise group consciousness about needed outreach efforts.

Collaboration between consumers and professionals presupposes that equity is possible and that traditional ways of interacting can be altered. Having been trained to cure, to advise, and to answer questions, many professionals have difficulty accepting a different role in relation to people they are accustomed to helping. Some professionals may have problems setting aside their training and seeing patients or clients as partners in a new arena where they are part of the solution instead of part of the problem.

On the other hand, assisting to start a support group provides professionals with an opportunity to help consumers overcome a sense of intimidation that in medical settings comes with the territory. With no desk, no white coat, and no clipboard to help them keep their distance, professionals can find another way to work with consumers in a new role in the group. Consumers, too, will discover their new role as equal partners with professionals.

THE MISSION STATEMENT

When people come together to meet common needs, it is a challenge to agree on the best way to meet them. From the outset, it helps if everyone involved shares a vision of what kind of organization they want to build. Leaders, whether self-appointed or elected, must invest time at the beginning and also take time as the group evolves to write a mission statement and set down their vision. These are more than academic exercises; they are opportunities to get in touch with the heart and soul of the group.

Both the mission statement and the vision need to be backed up by values. It is not enough to do the right thing; it must be done the right way. For example, it should be agreed that everyone will be treated with respect, that all personal exchanges will be treated with confidentiality, and that no one will pass judgment on another.

A mission statement tells people why the group exists. It is a concise, reader-friendly, public description of the organization's purpose. By taking the time to develop a mission statement, a group forces itself to focus on what need they are filling in society. There is usually so much to do that new groups rarely take the time to set their direction. The result can be frustration, disappointment, anger, or even failure—hardly the desired outcome, particularly for well-intentioned people who want to make things better.

If one person sees the group's purpose as providing peer support to individuals affected by a particular disease and another person sees it as raising money strictly for research, there is potential for conflict unless there are sufficient resources, human and financial, to support both kinds of programs. A mission statement serves as a touchstone for deciding which programs should be developed to further the purpose of the organization. The mission statements of three well-established support groups are as follows:

Muscular Dystrophy Association is a voluntary health agency working to defeat 40 neuromuscular diseases through programs of worldwide research, comprehensive patient and community services, and far-reaching professional and public health education.

The Crohn's and Colitis Foundation of America, Inc., is a nonprofit, research-oriented organization dedicated to finding the cause of, and cure for, Crohn's disease (ileitis) and ulcerative colitis. The Foundation is committed to a nationwide coordinated research program aimed at conquering these chronic and devastating intestinal diseases, which continue to baffle medical science.

MUMS is a national parent-to-parent organization for parents or care providers of a child with any disability, disorder, chromosomal abnormality or health condition. MUMS' main purpose is to provide support to parents in the form of a networking system that matches parents with other parents whose children have the same or similar condition.

The group's vision, on the other hand, describes what the group sees itself doing in the future: "In five years, this group will be the respected political voice for every family affected with ____ in the United States." "By the year 2000, we will be an international federation of families and professionals recognized as the most credible source of public information about ____." Doing a vision check at regular intervals is important, because groups, like people, continue to grow, and growth often means change. When leaders don't share a vision of where they want to go and what they want to be, they ultimately come into conflict. Guided by a shared vision, leaders have an easier time making those inevitable tough decisions that can so easily tear a group apart.

Perhaps most important, the vision must be shared and the purpose of the group must have personal meaning to the members, or they won't be members for long.

HOW TO AVOID PITFALLS

Learning from others is a fundamental concept in support groups, and it applies to groups as well as to individuals. Polly and John Arango have collected much sage advice over more than twenty-five years as part of New Mexico Parents Reaching Out. They offer the following guidelines to help avoid serious pitfalls:

- Organize around a specific issue. A group formed for some vague purpose, such as "to improve relations between parents and professionals," is much less likely to succeed than a group whose goal is, say, "to double the number of medically fragile children receiving nursing and other essential medical services in their own home."

- Make certain the organization's purpose is clear. If you cannot describe the purpose of your group in a few words, you're in trouble.

- Select your strategies (general ways to achieve your purpose) with great care. *Strategy* is a fancy word for figuring out how to make sure the person you are trying to influence will make the desired decision. Picking the right strategy will not necessarily ensure success, but it will certainly make your life easier. Choose strategies that suit your community, your target, and the members of your group.

- Avoid detailed planning. Instead, stick to your strategy and watch for chances to capitalize on opportunities as they develop. Too much detailed planning produces overly rigid organizations that cannot respond quickly to changing situations or promising alternatives.

- Start work on your issue at once. Spend the absolute minimum amount of time on organizational details. Once you know what you want or need to do, you will have to figure out how to get it done. You'll have to raise funds to pay for mailings, brochures, telephone, and so on. To get tax-deductible donations, you will need to incorporate and apply for nonprofit status as a public charity. Sometimes called a 501(c)(3), which refers to the applicable section of the Internal Revenue Code, a not-for-profit organization must serve a public purpose: religious, educational, charitable, scientific, cultural, or literary. The group must meet all IRS requirements, which include having bylaws and a board of directors. To qualify for the IRS exemption, you'll need to incorporate, write by-laws, and establish a board of directors. *But let organizational structure be an outgrowth of your work, not an obstacle to getting started.*

- Let your leaders emerge from your group. One reason for starting work before the actual structure of your group is set is to permit leaders to emerge from the actual work of the group.

- Find a role for everyone who wants to help. Don't worry about ideological purity; if someone is willing to help, put that person to work.

- Match the people to the work. There really are things that parents (consumers) do better than professionals, and things that professionals do better than consumers. Do not be afraid to reflect this fact in the way you assign tasks within your group. But do not put too much emphasis on roles; find and exploit what each person in the group does best.

  If no one volunteers for a certain task, there is usually one individual who feels compelled to make sure the work gets done anyway. It is not unusual to find the founder serving as the president/executive director, newsletter editor, and all-around do-it-all. This all too common tendency is a surefire prescription for burnout, and it can prove counterproductive. One person who does it all can discourage others from participating. Further, if no one volunteers to assume a particular responsibility, it may mean that the task or project is not important to anyone in the group and should be looked at again in terms of its relevance.

- Don't worry about how many people are active in the organization. Do worry about whether the organization is achieving its purpose.

- All organizations need to be nurtured and supported. Pay attention to the health of your organization. Make sure the members feel that their work is appreciated (and useful).

- Do not try to sustain an organization beyond its useful life. When the job is done, consider getting rid of the organization. It is easier to rally people around a new organization with a new purpose than to sustain an old organization until the right issue comes along.

— 5 —

Communications
and Publications

This "Mom and Pop" organization grew from the seed of a
dream . . . into an international organization that now has
1700 members in 22 countries and has 22 state chapters. I feel
we are a family to be proud of! What I'm most proud of is that
we have kept the true essence of a self-help group during our
growth. I've seen many special interest groups, in their desire
to raise money and expand, lose sight of what they were all
about in the first place. Yes, we are slowly growing, but a
strong foundation is being laid for the generations to come. As
a member, no matter what "growth stage" we are in, we need
to remember that we are a family committed to taking care of
each other, and bonded by the blood, sweat, and tears of
dealing with Prader-Willi syndrome.

J. TOMASESKI-HEINEMANN
The Gathered View: Newsletter of the
Prader-Willi Syndrome Association

As a group evolves, it becomes obvious that there are different
messages needed to reach different people for different reasons.
Naturally, people affected by a genetic disorder and their families
want as much information as they can get about the specific condition and related research and treatment. To the extent that they
perceive it as helpful, they may also want to know about coping with
the same disorder.

The key to effective communication is sharing meaningful
information in understandable language on a regular and timely
basis. A group that has something to say uses any means available to

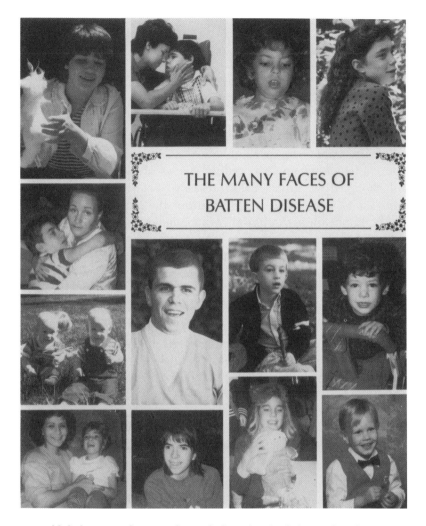

Beyond labels: Printed materials can help individuals know that they are not alone. (Batten's Disease Support and Research Association)

connect with the people who want to hear it. Content is more important than context. So is timing. In other words, a handwritten letter copied on white paper sent monthly might be more effective than a beautifully designed twelve-page publication with color photographs, different-colored inks, and fancy paper that is published only once a year.

If a genetic disorder is rare, it is probable that people who share concerns are scattered. A newsletter, telephone network, or computer bulletin board may offer the most immediate link among members.

A FEW BASICS

Information about the group should appear in all of its publications. The bare essentials include the name and address of the group, a telephone contact, and the names of the board of directors and the medical or scientific advisory board. This information helps establish credibility and positions the group as a reliable resource. Publications should always be dated, so readers know how current they are.

Computers have greatly simplified the production of printed pieces. A volunteer with a basic knowledge of desktop publishing can produce materials that are attractive and inexpensive to reproduce. Software programs like WordPerfect and Microsoft Word have gone beyond word processing and now include templates that make it easy to create professional-looking letters, memos, fliers, and newsletters. Harvard Graphics, Microsoft Publisher, and Aldus Pagemaker are among the better-known publishing programs.

In addition to being able to design and typeset publications on the computer, groups now have a great variety of preprinted papers to choose from. Companies like PaperDirect (100 Plaza Drive, Secaucus, NJ 07094-3606, phone 800 APAPERS) sell small quantities of high-quality, multicolored stock, which can make the plainest announcement, invitation, or publication into an eye-catching public relations tool. Large stationery stores have copied this idea and are now offering their own brand of specialty papers.

NEWSLETTERS

A newsletter sent through the mail is the most direct way to reach the most people. It is important to limit the scope of a newsletter so that regular production does not become an overwhelming task. There is a direct correlation between costs, in terms of time and money, and the burden felt by the volunteer responsible for getting a newsletter out. Be aware that the bigger and more comprehensive a publication is, the longer it takes to get done. In the meantime, readers may not get the information they want when they need it. In addition, opportunities for involving readers with the group are lost.

It is useful to build a mailing list and analyze it before deciding on the contents of a newsletter. There are preliminary questions to address. What information will readers want? Where will that information come from? Are there experts who will volunteer to write articles? Will one individual or a committee review the material for accuracy? Should all the material be written in lay language? If the readers are primarily consumers, articles should be written in language that the majority of readers can understand and that is free of medical terms and jargon. A word of caution: in the interest of simplicity, accuracy could be compromised; editors without medical expertise should ask the group's medical advisors to review articles containing scientific information (Bennett, 1990). In essence, four basic questions need to be asked:

- Who needs the information, and where are people going to get information?
- What format will reach your target audience most effectively?
- What other materials exist that address the same subject?
- What do you want to happen after your information reaches your target audience?

For some groups, a newsletter is the only way families have of communicating with each other. They share personal experiences as well as opinions on a range of topics such as treatments, medications, emotional and psychological effects, adoption, home care, and even caregivers.

If the mailing list includes professionals, families need to know. Many professionals read group newsletters to gain more insight into family needs and to have access to thoughts and feelings that may never be shared in a clinical setting. While the information is used to help professionals work more successfully with families, some families may be uncomfortable disclosing their feelings in a public forum with a circulation wider than the group's members.

A Scientist Speaks Out on Brain Specimen Shortage

The TSA Brain Bank Program is emerging as one of the most useful resources in the study of Tourette Syndrome. Why it is so vital to future progress is discussed by **George M. Anderson, Ph.D.** *of the Child Study Center, Yale University School of Medicine.*

As a research neuroscientist interested in finding the causes of Tourette Syndrome, I am constantly considering the question: how does one best attempt to understand the brain alteration present in individuals with Tourette Syndrome? The answer seems clear: one carries out detailed, careful and extensive studies of postmortem brain tissue of people who had Tourette Syndrome.

There are two reasons to believe postmortem brain research provides one of the best approaches. First, literally every day we are learning more about the structure and function of the brain. The extremely rapid advances in neuroscience means that we are able to make better and better measurements of more and more aspects of the human brain. This is true for every level that the brain

is studied, including the molecular, neurochemical, cellular and anatomical. Not only are we able to assess the brain more completely, but we can also make more informed decisions about which aspects of the brain should be studied in greatest detail.

Secondly, the postmortem brain tissue approach has proved to be very revealing about the alterations present in Parkinsonism, Huntington's Disease, and Alzheimer's. In fact this research has been the single most influential factor contributing to our understanding of those conditions. The current treatments for those disorders, and the therapies now being tested rest in great measure on the findings from our vastly improved understanding due to brain tissue research. For example, when we read about patients with Parkinson's Disease receiving the dopaminergic pharmacotherapy, or having dopamine-producing cells transplanted into their striatum, or the potential of gene therapy through transferring genes for dopamine-producing enzymes, we should know that these breakthroughs are based on the postmortem findings of reduced levels of the neurotransmitter dopamine in the brains of Parkinson's Disease patients.

With Tourette Syndrome there are a number of intriguing hypotheses about the chemical imbalance in the brain that causes the symptoms. The only way to examine these specific ideas is by examining the brain chemically. And for this we need specimens. Unfortunately, there continues to be a real shortage of appropriate tissue to study. The dedication of TSA in recruiting potential donors is to be applauded. It is difficult to overstate the importance of these registration efforts, and impossible to overestimate the value of the postmortem brain tissue we in the scientific community so urgently need.

New TSA Brain Bank Brochure to Be Distributed

There is one machine that weighs just three pounds, contains ten billion working parts, functions by chemistry, electricity and means not yet fully understood, and can casually perform acts that make even the most modern super-computer seem primitive.

It is the human brain. Sometimes, however, it is mysteriously mis-wired...

Who should register with the TSA Brain Bank program? How would I go about it? Does registering involve any costs to me? If I want more information, whom should I call?

These questions — and more — are answered in a new TSA Brain Bank brochure soon to be mailed to every person on TSA's mailing list. Additional copies for family members are available from TSA free of charge.

As you read through the clear, brief text, you will come to realize more keenly the widespread benefit from just one single donation of brain tissue that can provide urgently needed tissue samples for hundreds of scientists. Included are a registration form and wallet-size donor cards.

Because brain tissue is stored permanently, many registrants view this as an appropriate, lasting memorial. Please look for your copy, read it over, and then give serious consideration to registering with this vital TSA program.

--- Clip and Save ---

HELP SCIENTISTS FIND THE CURE...

When brain tissue donations are to be made, a family member or friend must call, without delay, to the nearest Brain Bank. All banks receive calls 24 hours a day.

Eastern U.S. McLean Hospital Brain Tissue Resource Center	800-BRAIN BANK (800-272-4622)
Western U.S. National Neurological Research Bank	(310) 824-4307 M-F 8:30 am-6:00 pm PST (310) 478-3711 all other times
Canada Canadian Brain Tissue Bank	(416) 977-3398

The caller should provide the name of the medical professional to be contacted, and the name and location of the hospital, nursing home or funeral home.

For TSA Brain Bank registration kits call (718) 224-2999.

TSA gratefully acknowledges

the generosity of

PANORAMA PRESS

and **M&M BINDERY**

for the printing

of the Newsletter

The Tourette Syndrome Association used their newsletter as an effective vehicle for educating readers about the TSA Brain Bank. On a single, well-designed page, an article by an expert in the field documents the need for brain tissue research and provides background information to support a new brochure being distributed to the public. (Tourette Syndrome Association, Inc.)

As a group grows, a newsletter can function to sustain members' interest, to involve and educate professionals, and to demonstrate the value of programs to funders. If a newsletter has regular columns, readers may more easily find information that interests them. If it is more than four pages in length, the newsletter should include a table of contents in the front, and each page should be numbered.

A message from the president or executive director is an opportunity to summarize activities and to motivate people to get more involved. It also affords an important and public way to say thank you. In the following example, the executive director of K. S. and Associates strikes the right balance in her warm and welcoming column:

> Hello, peoples! This is a phrase that our fourteen-year-old son uses around the house. It's his "I feel good and how are you doing on this fine day?" comment. I think I'm going to borrow it for this issue's newsletter. We have so many good things to report in this issue: the new ALZA patch is out, we have news about a promising study going on in southern California concerning long-acting injectables, there are some well-thought-out questions and answers in the "Ask the Doctor" column and a very instructional article on why and how testosterone works. We would like to share with you news from around the country on support group meetings that have occurred in the past few months. Be sure and read about our first national Klinefelter Syndrome and Associates Conference. If you are in a position to help with this conference, drop us a line. (Aylstock, 1994, 1)

Some newsletters focus on specific interest groups. For example, *Parents' Forum* is published by Little People of America specifically for the parents of children with dwarfism. It also includes articles geared to the concerns of grandparents. The National Down Syndrome Society underwrites a publication written by and for young adults. One of the contributors describes its origin: "My family has been getting the Down syndrome newsletter since I was very small and I slowly began to learn a little about Down syndrome. When I was 7 or 8 years old I didn't like the meaning of Down. So I began to cross out the 'Down' and write 'Up' on the newsletter. . . . I think that it is very important for everybody to be 'Up' people if they would like to be happy and have lots of friends. I don't think people want to be friendly with other people who are not happy. Also we should always keep trying to do new things even if we cannot do them well" (Forts, 1994, 11–12).

DISCLAIMERS, PERMISSIONS, AND READER SURVEYS

It is a good idea to publish a disclaimer in each issue of a newsletter. Organizations that publish materials from many sources want readers to know that the opinions expressed do not represent the organization. This disclaimer is particularly important when dealing with issues around which there is controversy, such as abortion, adoption, carrier screening, and experimental treatments. Groups can disagree about the carrier rate of a genetic disorder. They might differ on the efficacy of a new therapy. It is wise to acknowledge differences of opinion and to try to present balanced information so readers can make their own informed decisions.

The International Rett Syndrome Association *Newsletter* includes the following policy statement, which offers a good model:

> In an effort to improve the quality of life for our daughters with Rett Syndrome, we welcome ideas from our readers on various techniques of management and care, general and educational suggestions that individuals have investigated and/or found beneficial. This exchange of ideas is welcome. Parents and others have the opportunity to decide if they want to follow through with the suggestions.
>
> We do not, however, as an organization, support or endorse any particular treatment, therapy, or medication. We encourage parents to support one another with suggestions and to contact their child's physician for final approval.

A photograph release gives permission to use an individual's photograph. The wording can be simple: "I give ____ my permission to publish a photograph showing [describe the contents of the photo], taken [date and place], in [name of publication]. The publisher does/does not have permission to identify me in the photograph."

Remember that there is a fine line between education and exploitation that is easily crossed in the zeal to promote a good cause. Individuals have strong feelings about being publicly identified with a genetic disorder. Issues of privacy and confidentiality must be considered at all times, particularly when developing materials for public consumption.

Occasional reader surveys are useful for evaluating the effectiveness of a newsletter. Readers should be encouraged to let the editor know which topics are of greatest interest. Many groups include a regular section where families can share their experiences and ask questions. The more involved readers are, the more they are likely to support the group in other ways.

ACKNOWLEDGMENT OF FINANCIAL AND RESOURCE CONTRIBUTIONS

Many newsletters list financial contributions. This public form of acknowledgment is an acceptable method of fund-raising and serves as a model by letting readers know of opportunities to contribute. Contributions given in memory or honor of someone are listed on a regular basis. Some groups publish a listing by category once a year. For example: Angels ($1,000 and up), Benefactors ($500–$999), Sponsors ($100–$499), Friends ($50–$99).

A newsletter should be considered an actual program, and it can be funded by outside sources. A local business may give a restricted donation to cover all the costs. On the other hand, in-kind contributions instead of cash from several sources can also get the job done. A local printer, copy shop, or large company with heavy-duty copying capacity may be a likely potential provider of reproduction services. Some groups get the paper from one source and graphic design (including typesetting) from another.

All contributors to the publication should be listed. Acknowledgments not only serve as a thank you but also keep all relationships in the open, lessening concerns about possible conflicts of interest.

MAILING OPTIONS

It is easy to forget to factor in volunteer time spent addressing and mailing newsletters when calculating the costs associated with this program. However, these functions add up. Several ways of mailing are cheaper than first class, but saving money in postage may cost more in preparation and delivery time. Once a list grows beyond two hundred names, a newsletter can be mailed third-class bulk rate. Because the level of presorting that the mail receives determines the rate, the finer the sort, the more money is saved. All mail must be sorted by zip code and bundled before it is delivered to the post office, and it can take up to three weeks to be delivered.

Nonprofit organizations are eligible to mail third class at special low rates. To qualify, the group must meet certain requirements with both the Internal Revenue Service and the U.S. Postal Service. There is a one-time fee to the Postal Service for a bulk rate number and an annual fee for the right to mail without affixing postage. Many groups maintain their own lists and handle the preparation of mailings. Others use a mail service or a full-service letter shop to print and mail for them. When it comes to maintaining a mailing list and generating labels in a specific order, computers can help save time and money. There are many software programs for mailing list management, including Filemaker Pro. *Third-Class Mail Preparation* (publication 49, May 1993), available from the Postal Service, contains clear instructions for using third-class mail. The Postal Service also offers a video guide, called *Ten or More,* to third-class mail preparation.

A word of caution: Mailing lists are valuable. Many people would like to have access to the names that organizers work so hard to gather. To protect the privacy of families, groups should develop a policy with regard to the sharing or selling of lists. There are other options. For example, if a company is promoting a product of interest to members or if people are needed for a research study, the information can be published in a newsletter or disseminated by inserting a special flier.

COMMUNICATION BY
COMPUTER NETWORKING

Although electronic communication via computer opens up the possibility of sending messages around the world and promises instant contact, not everyone has access to this technology. Moreover, not everyone who has a computer has mastered the effective use of communication networks such as the Internet.

New technologies are increasingly being used by consumers to find medical information, advice, and support. A new field called consumer health informatics is devoted to the study, development, and implementation of computer and telecommunications applications and interfaces designed for use by health consumers. Ed

Madara, director of the American Self-Help Clearinghouse, is a knowledgeable advocate of computer communications. He envisions a situation where computers will bring together people who might otherwise never be able to be part of a support group. At the First National Consumer Health Informatics Conference, held in 1993, he shared his vision of a world linked by computer:

> With time, more affordable computers, and the inevitable development of integrated telephone-TV-information-home entertainment systems, more people will be participating in mutual aid efforts and self-help communities. High tech is doing this by enabling people to overcome some of the traditional problems: lack of an existing local group to attend, lack of transportation or time available for travel, rarity of the condition, and most limitations of physical disability. Community centers, social service agencies, and public libraries can provide needed orientation and access to computers for those who cannot afford them. Overall, computers will revolutionize society, increasing the linkage of people, ideas and concerns on national and international levels. [A] better understanding and use of these empowering tools and networks will both promote a new form of community and . . . accelerate the natural cycle of social and health change—helping people to more quickly and readily network, organize, educate or advocate to meet their needs.

According to Madara, all that is necessary is a personal computer, a modem, and a telecommunications software program to access hundreds of free bulletin board systems (BBSs). These bulletin boards are a place for exchanging messages and, for many users, are a convenient way to go beyond the bounds of traditional face-to-face support groups. A phone listing of more than three hundred health-related BBSs is available for $5 from Ed Del Grosso, P.O. Box 632, Collegeville, PA 19426. Those who are already computer competent may call Del Grosso's Black Bag BBS at (610) 454-7396 to download the listing.

National commercial computer networks, like America OnLine, CompuServe, and Delphi, charge a monthly fee for a specified number of hours of use. Through such commercial networks, individuals can participate in online group meetings or search extensive library files for information on specific disorders, including symp-

FRAXA

Research Foundation, Inc.

P.O. Box 935
West Newbury, MA 01985
(508) 462-1990

*dedicated to improving the lives of
individuals with Fragile X Syndrome
by speeding progress towards
effective treatment*

*"As a parent of two children
with Fragile X, I can imagine no
greater dream than the
knowledge to treat their illness.
Scientific research is the tool
with which to grasp this dream."*

-- Katherine Clapp, parent

FRAXA

Research Foundation, Inc.

*A nonprofit, tax-exempt organization
run by volunteer parents of children
with fragile X syndrome*

Mass. Chapter/Headquarters
P.O. Box 935
West Newbury, MA 01985
phone: (508) 462-1990-0935
email: fraxa@destek.net

New York Chapter
P.O. Box 520
Ardsley, NY 10502-0520
phone: (914) 674-4480
fax: (914) 674-4540

Virginia Chapter
P.O. Box 53
Fairfax Station, VA 22039
phone: (703) 278-9144

FRAXA

Research Foundation, Inc.

*promoting research for
the treatment of*

Fragile **X** Syndrome

*one of the most common
inherited diseases worldwide
yet virtually unknown!*

Above and on facing page: *The publication of a brochure marks an important step in establishing the credibility of a new group. FRAXA Research Foundation designed their trifold brochure to fit on a standard piece of 8½" x 11" paper, which is printed on both sides. (FRAXA Research Foundation)*

toms, causes, affected population, standard therapies, current experimental therapies, research projects, and organizational resources. Subscribers to CompuServe can access the National Organization for Rare Disorders's Rare Disease Database. There is also a growing number of specialty networks for professionals, such as MCH-Net for maternal and child health care workers.

If the goal is to get on the "information highway," the publication *Electronic Networking for Nonprofit Groups* (funded by the Benton Foundation, Apple Community Affairs, and the Telecommunications Education Trust) provides a good road map for pioneers. Find a local computer resource for face-to-face guidance or contact the American Self-Help Clearinghouse for more specifics.

In addition to opening up new communication pathways, a computer is the best way to handle tedious record keeping and the maintenance of lists. However, any box that can hold index cards can

What is Fragile X?

Fragile X Syndrome causes a host of symptoms which can vary widely from one individual to the next.

- mental impairment
- Attention Deficit Hyperactivity Disorder
- anxiety and unstable mood
- long face, large ears, and double-jointed fingers

Boys are typically more affected than girls: 99% of boys have mental retardation.

Although Fragile X is as common as Down Syndrome, it is virtually unknown. More common than cystic fibrosis or muscular dystrophy, Fragile X is often misdiagnosed.

Who Gets Fragile X?

Anyone can unknowingly carry Fragile X!

Fragile X is caused by a mutation of a gene on the X chromosome. Both men and women can carry the gene and pass it to their children. The mutation can lurk silently in families for centuries before affecting a child. A blood test can detect Fragile X in carriers and affected individuals.

- 1 in 1000 people are affected
- 1 in 400 women are carriers, passing the gene to 50% of their children

Will there be Treatment?

Gene therapy and protein replacement hold great promise for the treatment of Fragile X.

In Fragile X Syndrome, a mutation in a single gene causes the gene to shut down. Like a defective factory, the gene cannot build its protein product. If the gene or its product could be replaced in the cells of the brain, the disease could be treated.

The entire gene therapy field is progressing rapidly. However, research is needed on ways to adapt gene therapy techniques for treatment of brain disorders. To date, the brain has been largely ignored.

We believe that this research will directly benefit those who suffer from Fragile X Syndrome, Huntington's disease, Parkinson's disease, Alzheimer's disease, and many other neuropsychiatric disorders.

"The fact that Fragile X is a single gene disorder makes the probability of finding an effective treatment for the current generation of affected children much more likely. I think a reasonable time frame needed to develop a rational treatment for Fragile X is about 5 years."

-- W. Ted Brown, MD, PhD

Chief, Department of Human Genetics Institute for Basic Research in Developmental Disabilities, Staten Island, NY

What is FRAXA?

The FRAXA Research Foundation, Inc. is a non-profit corporation founded this year by parents of children with Fragile X to:

- promote scientific research for the treatment of Fragile X Syndrome by funding promising research.
- Increase public awareness of Fragile X

FRAXA's goal is an effective treatment available by the year 2000. Donations to FRAXA are fully tax-deductible.

FRAXA Board of Directors

Katherine Clapp *President*
Parent, Adjunct Professor of Computer Science
Newburyport, MA

Justine Juarez
Dean of Continuing Education, Merrimack College, North Andover, MA

Lars Lundgren, M.D.
Pediatrician, Newburyport, MA

Kathleen May *Vice President*
Parent; Legislative Advocate, ARC of N. Virginia

Pamela Mellon, Ph.D.
Professor of Reproductive Medicine & Neuroscience, Univ. of California at San Diego

Michael Tranfaglia, M.D.
Treasurer/Secretary/ Medical Director
Psychopharmacologist, Parent, Newburyport MA

do the job. It may be more professional to generate letters and to design newsletters on a computer, but the power of the old-fashioned pen should not be underestimated. The lack of high-tech equipment should not become an obstacle. Regardless of the way a group communicates, constant communication should be a high priority.

EDUCATIONAL MATERIALS FOR THE PUBLIC AND PROFESSIONALS

To reach a broad public, it is necessary to develop written materials that serve specific functions: a brochure about the group and the disorder, a fact sheet, and a handbook for different kinds of professionals, such as primary care physicians or school nurses. Some groups produce educational videotapes.

Assisting in the development of educational materials is a meaningful role for members of a medical or scientific advisory board, and their involvement can raise the comfort level of professionals who may not be familiar with the group and its mission. Establishing this credibility with professionals is critical if they are ever going to refer new families to the group. It is advisable, therefore, to work with professionals (including genetic counselors, social workers, nurses, researchers, and physicians) to ensure that the information is correct. These professionals can also play a key role in the distribution of materials.

Most groups focus on developing materials but do not plan adequately for their distribution. Nor do they consider ways to evaluate their effectiveness. The need to reach out is a constant pressure fueled by personal experiences of frustration and isolation. Sadly, countless people have told tales about the difficulty of getting accurate information when they needed it most. Many have horror stories of misinformation that make a compelling and urgent case for getting the word out. Such a pressing responsibility can quickly become overwhelming and lead to scattered efforts that do little more than burn out volunteers and burn up scant resources. It pays to take the time to ask some preliminary questions, whose answers can help determine priorities.

Who Needs the Information?
Where Can People Get Information?

To reach families, consider different points of contact: specialists, pediatricians, hospital nurses, medical social workers, coalitions such as the National Organization for Rare Disorders or the Alliance of Genetic Support Groups, the public library, popular publications, television, and radio. To reach physicians, weigh the benefits and compare the costs of a direct mailing to individuals with those of exhibiting at a national meeting where you can engage professionals in a dialogue and give out materials.

Sometimes there are barriers to getting information to people that must be overcome. The National Tay-Sachs and Allied Diseases Association has a four-page brochure to inform the public about Tay-Sachs disease. It describes the disorder, the populations at greatest risk, and testing programs. When two waves of immigration brought thousands of Russian Jews to the United States, the organization recognized the need to translate their brochure and make it available through social service agencies working with large groups of these new Americans. By frequently evaluating this one educational piece, the organization found a solution to a problem that could have diminished the effectiveness of their outreach. They identified an appropriate distribution mechanism and, consequently, reached the people who needed the information they had to offer.

Trisomy 18: A Book for Families contains a clear statement of purpose. Written by two genetic counselors—the founder of the Support Organization for Trisomy 18/13 and a pediatric geneticist—this work targets families whose children have recently been diagnosed with trisomy 18 or trisomy 13. The contents include a glossary of terms as well as a listing of resources for families.

Some publications address families, professionals, and others interested in the particular genetic disorder all at once. For example, *Fragile X Syndrome: A Handbook for Families and Professionals* was designed "as a guide for families, counselors, caretakers, educators, and all those wishing to learn about fragile X syndrome" (Finucane, McCoonkie-Rosell, and Cronister, 1993). It successfully combines a description of the syndrome, how it is inherited, and diagnostic testing methods, with family case studies illustrating the impact of the disorder on families. Quotations from parents, illustrations, photographs, and charts enrich the text, which ends with a brief description of the National Fragile X Foundation. Other materials target a special segment of the population. *What Is Thalassemia?* by the Cooley's Anemia Foundation, for example, talks to older thalassemic patients to help them understand their disease, the reasons for their treatment, and the hope for their future (Vullo and Modell, 1990).

Sometimes, a publication can have cross-disability value. Huntington's Disease Society of America has produced a booklet for people wishing to develop a Huntington's-disease-related support group as well as for the leaders and participants of established groups (Greene, 1992). Although created as a service to one organization's constituency, the booklet contains much general information that can be used by anyone interested in starting and sustaining a support group. It is a well-written, hands-on guide that benefits greatly from the contributions of many professionals and laypeople.

Occasionally, a book such as *Little People in America: The Social Dimensions of Dwarfism* (Ablon, 1984, p. ix) is written by an interested professional author and published with the approval of the voluntary genetics organization. A well-known anthropologist who

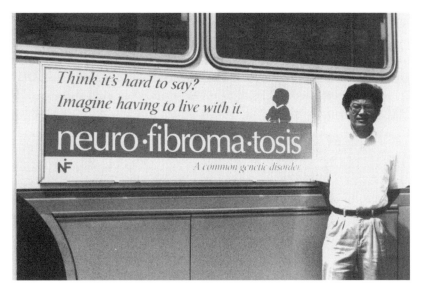

From T-shirts to bus panels, consider every possible medium to deliver your message. (National Neurofibromatosis Foundation)

had attended several national conferences of Little People of America recognized a gap and filled it:

> There exists no book that doctors, nurses, physical therapists, social workers, or other health or social service professionals who work with dwarfs can read to learn about the special kinds of life experiences that help to shape their patients' and clients' lives and their perceptions about themselves as totally functioning individuals. There is no book that the parents of a dwarf child can read to give them an understanding of the kinds of lives that they and their child may anticipate and plan for. There exists no book that dwarfs, many of whom feel that they are unique in their condition and the events of their lives, can read to learn what others like themselves have undergone.

What Format Will Most Effectively Reach the Target Audience?

Given time and financial constraints, hard choices must be made. Is it better to invest in printing and mailing a thousand brochures to a

---

October is Rett Syndrome Awareness Month

By Ro Vargo & Paul Jochim

At the IRSA Board of Directors meeting last fall, it was decided to develop a plan to increase Rett syndrome awareness. A committee was formed called the Rett Syndrome Awareness and Collaboration Committee. Ro Vargo and Paul Jochim are co-chairpersons. This will be a collaborative effort with everyone interested in Rett syndrome participating—the general membership of IRSA, all Rett syndrome support groups, associations, and foundations in the United States and worldwide.

The goal of this committee is to inform and educate others about Rett syndrome. Through awareness comes understanding, concern, support, and recognition of the syndrome and its uniqueness. We have chosen October as the month to start this annual campaign because our girls are in school and new teachers may be working with them for the first time. Many parent/teacher conferences will be held in the fall.

We need your ideas and input on how we can best do this and your commitment

to help us in your area in October. Here are some ideas we have already:

1. Tell five people about Rett syndrome and give them a brochure.
2. Send out Rett syndrome brochures to your doctors.
3. Call your local library and ask them if they have any books on Rett syndrome. Tell them about Barbro Lindberg's book *Understanding Rett Syndrome.*
4. Ask your school's special education department if they have Barbro Lindberg's book, *Understanding Rett Syndrome.*
5. Call your local college, hospital and agencies that provide services for the disabled.
6. Ask to speak to your local Women's Club, Jaycees, Lions, or other service organizations.
7. Call or write dictionary and encyclopedia publishers and ask them to include Rett syndrome in their publications.
8. Call your local newspaper, radio, or television station. Tell them about Rett Syndrome Awareness Month and your family. Ask them if they would do a

story. We are trying to find girls who are misdiagnosed or undiagnosed and reach out to them and their families.
9. Organize a walk-a-thon to raise awareness and money for Rett syndrome research. There are countless other projects that you can do. Pick one that you like.
10. Ask your Mayor or Governor to issue a proclamation
11. Obtain wallet-sized cards from IRSA for people who want more information on Rett syndrome.
12. Ask to speak at a School Board meeting about Rett syndrome. They usually have time at the start of the meeting for comments. You can say a lot in two or three minutes.

More information will be available at this year's conference and in the summer newsletter. Please let us know your suggestions and ideas about what you can do. We encourage you to become involved and help make a difference. Let's make everyone aware that "October is Rett Syndrome Awareness Month!"

Outreach takes many forms. By focusing activities on public awareness during a special month each year, groups can involve volunteers by offering a diverse list of opportunities. (International Rett Syndrome Association) purchased list of neurologists or to work to ensure that every class graduating from a local medical school has met a family and heard their story? Perhaps more people can be reached by writing a thirty-second public service announcement and mailing it to radio stations in major markets than by trying to interest a national television program in featuring a single disorder. Will a young mother be more likely to read a brochure in the doctor's office or to watch a five-minute videotape?

What Other Materials Exist that Address the Same Subject?

In this age of information, it is wise to devote time to researching what materials are currently available about specific disorders before starting to develop yet another. It may turn out that, rather than creating a new brochure, the group might help circulate materials already in print. Much time and energy can be saved by building on materials that may only need updating.

Whether starting from scratch or not, it is wise to be aware of what else is available. A genetic counselor or a contact at a genetics center, which can usually be found in a major university-based medical center, will probably be willing to do a literature search. The coordinators of the regional genetics networks are knowledge-able about materials and can be of assistance (see Appendix B). The Alliance of Genetic Support Groups can provide the name and tele-phone number of the genetics coordinator in each state. This indi-vidual is not only a good contact but also a vital link to genetics professionals close to home who are usually glad to provide assis-tance. Resources vary from state to state. The Genetic Disease Branch of the California State Department of Health Services, for example, houses a resource center called GeneHELP, composed of a database of more than 430 titles of materials on genetic diseases, hemoglo-binopathies, birth defects, newborn screening, and prenatal diagno-sis. Materials are reviewed by a staff of consumers, teachers, health educators, doctors, genetic counselors, and nurses. Single copies of specific titles are available. Currently, the service is available only to California health care providers; however, an effort is under way to make the GeneHELP database nationally accessible to others through Internet.

All the preliminary research has value, regardless of the results. If the search yields nothing, at least a real need has been documented. If materials are identified, then precious time and energy have been saved.

What Should Happen after Information Reaches the Target Audience?

Is the purpose to connect with new families? To increase donations? To get more people to join? To make readers better informed? Expectations must be clear, otherwise it will be difficult to evaluate the usefulness of the material or to know if the piece is effective. Consequently, there will be no way to judge whether or not the time and money invested were well spent. Equally important, it will not be possible to assess whether or not the material contains what the target audience wants and really needs.

The VHL Handbook, a reference handbook for patients with von Hippel-Lindau disease, their families, and support personnel, contains a feedback sheet with open-ended questions about what readers like and what they want changed or added. Such an evaluation tool is useful if a significant number are returned. Alternative methods are a telephone survey of known recipients or a focus group. A great deal can be learned by asking the right questions before you start developing an educational piece and again when you have completed it.

PUBLICIZING YOUR PUBLICATIONS

There are several ways to advertise the availability of an educational publication without cost. Every regional genetics network has a newsletter that carries announcements of new materials. The Alliance of Genetic Support Groups lists new groups and new publications in its monthly publication, *Alert.* It is useful to send sample copies to genetics centers, genetic counselors, and other concerned professionals.

Once a group has more than one publication, it is time to create a publications list that can also serve as an order blank. A sample publications list might look like this (from *Turner Syndrome News,* Summer 1994):

The following materials are available through the Turner's Syndrome Society of the United States. Use the order form below to make your request.

Turner's Syndrome: A Guide for Families. An 18-page booklet to help families understand what Turner's syndrome is, what causes it, and how families can help girls with TS cope with their physical, social and emotional concerns. . . . No charge for single copies. $3.25 for multiple copies. Also available in Spanish.

Turner's Syndrome: A Guide for Families (Video). The doctor has just made the diagnosis. What does this mean for the future? 21 minutes. 1991. $15.00 per copy.

Turner's Syndrome: A Guide for Physicians. A 24-page booklet addressing the definition, etiology, clinical features, and management of Turner's Syndrome. No charge for single copies. $3.25 each for multiple copies.

Resource Bibliographies. A list of articles and publications addressing various aspects of TS. No charge.

Include a publications list in mailings and newsletters. By constantly reminding people about the availability of materials, groups can turn their materials into a steady source of income. Don't forget to charge for postage and handling. Ask an accountant for guidance about sales tax.

PRESS RELEASES AND PUBLIC SERVICE ANNOUNCEMENTS

A press release (or news release) is useful for informing the public about upcoming events. The release should be typed and double-spaced. The name of a contact and a telephone number should appear at the top of the first sheet. It is best to keep the announcement short and to the point: who, what, where, when, and why.

Radio stations will generally air a public service announcement (PSA) for a recognized nonprofit organization. PSAs, which can be fifteen, thirty, or sixty seconds long, are read as a community service and must be received by the station at a specified time before the date of the event.

WEINER AND ASSOCIATES

NEWS

<u>RELEASE ON RECEIPT</u>

<u>FREE TAY-SACHS TESTING TO BE OFFERED AT WALK-A-THON</u>

Free Tay-Sachs testing will be offered as part of the Children for Children Walk for Life Walk-a-thon to be held Sunday, October 4 (rain date October 11), from 1 to 4 p.m. at the Philadelphia Zoo, it was announced by co-chairpersons of the event Robin Goldman and Linda Rabinowitz.

"While the walk-a-thon to benefit National Tay-Sachs and Allied Diseases Association of Delaware Valley will be a fun-filled afternoon for everyone, as a special accommodation to those participating, as well as to anyone attending the zoo that day, free Tay-Sachs testing will be available from 1 to 4 p.m.," says Rabinowitz.

The simple blood test which is taken to determine carrier status is usually $30. Thousands of unsuspecting carriers and dozens of carrier couples have been uncovered through the Tay-Sachs Prevention Program at Thomas Jefferson University.

Registration fee for the walk-a-thon is $3 per participant and includes admission to the zoo. With a $5 minimum pledge per person or $10 per family, walkers will receive a Children for Children Walk for Life t-shirt. Adults who are not registered for the walk-a-thon, but wish to accompany walkers, will receive a $1 discount on the zoo's entrance fee.

Advance registration is requested. For registration information, please call the Tay-Sachs office at (215) 887-0877.

The Children for Children Walk for Life is jointly sponsored by the five branches of National Tay-Sachs and Allied Diseases Association of Delaware Valley.

more...

Marketing • Advertising
Public Relations
167 Deer Run Road
Willow Grove, PA 19090
(215) 657-1387
FAX: (215) 657-0146

This sample news release covers the basics: who, what, where, when, and why. (Weiner and Associates)

T-S 10/4 (add one)

Tay-Sachs is an inherited disease which strikes young children. It causes progressive destruction of the central nervous system and death by five years of age.

National Tay-Sachs and Allied Diseases Association is a nonprofit voluntary health agency devoted to the prevention of Tay-Sachs and the allied diseases through research, testing and education programs. The Tay-Sachs Prevention Program at Thomas Jefferson University is funded by NTSAD of Delaware Valley.

#

FOR FURTHER INFORMATION:
Rhoda Weiner
Weiner and Associates
(215) 657-1387   September 28, 1987

WEINER AND ASSOCIATES

Contact:	Rhoda Weiner
	(215) 657-1387
FAX:	(215) 657-0146

PUBLIC SERVICE ANNOUNCEMENT

TIME: 30 SECONDS

FOR USE: THROUGH OCTOBER 16

Are you expecting a baby? If so, you're probably thinking about a lot more than just painting the nursery.

Come to **Great Expectations: Planning a Healthy Pregnancy and Birth**, a free seminar at Methodist Hospital, 2301 South Broad Street, on Tuesday, October 16 from 7 to 8 p.m. A panel of experts will discuss prenatal care, pregnancy and childbirth.

It's all part of Jefferson's Women's Health Week. For further information, call 955-5671. That's 955-5671.

-30-

RJW 9/19/90

Marketing • Advertising
Public Relations
167 Deer Run Road
Willow Grove, PA 19090
(215) 657-1387
FAX: (215) 657-0146

Public service announcements are aired on the radio without charge. Local stations usually have a community affairs department that is responsible for handling this form of publicity. (Weiner and Associates)

—6—
Meetings and Major Program Areas

If you are starting a local group in an area where people live close enough to meet on a regular basis, you will want to maintain and increase their interest by stimulating as much individual involvement as possible. Think of each gathering as an opportunity for educating as well as networking and sharing.

A committee with specific assignments should address the basics: the place, the date and time, and the program. Each of these items can affect success.

SELECTING A MEETING PLACE AND A TIME TO MEET

Meeting space should be chosen with care. The first question is whether you want to meet in someone's home or in a more public place. Hospitals, libraries, community centers, churches, and synagogues frequently provide meeting rooms without charge to nonprofit groups. Some civic groups (such as the Lions or Kiwanis) may assist you if they have their own buildings. Other possible resources include family service agencies, the Red Cross, the Salvation Army, or senior centers. Sometimes groups hold meetings in an office conference room. Since the location can set the tone for the group, however, it is important to consider if an institutional setting like a hospital or the warmer atmosphere of a home is preferable.

You Are Not Alone: A Guide to Establishing HD Support Groups (Greene, 1992) identifies some good questions to consider when choosing a meeting place:

- Is it accessible to public and private transportation?
- Is there adequate parking? What is the parking fee?
- Is the neighborhood safe and well lit?
- Are the building and room wheelchair accessible?
- Is the size of the room adequate?
- Are there movable chairs that can be arranged in a circle? Are they comfortable?
- Is the room well lit? Is it well ventilated and acoustically adequate?
- Is it air-conditioned?
- Is there easy access to a bathroom?
- Is a telephone available to receive emergency calls?
- Can refreshments be brought into the facility? Is there an electrical outlet for making hot beverages? Are water and ice cubes available?
- Does the facility have a microphone and audiovisual equipment if these are needed for the meeting? If not, can they be brought into the facility?
- Are there tables that can be used for registration and refreshments?
- Who has a key to the room? Can it be obtained beforehand?

No place will be perfect, but it helps to eliminate known obstacles whenever possible. Likewise, no date or time will satisfy everyone. Flexibility and creativity should be active ingredients in all planning. The best you can do is to take into account people's preferences. A membership survey can tell you how many people work, a factor that might rule out daytime meetings. Where members live and health conditions affect how far they can travel.

It might be necessary to try different times, days, and formats. Many groups find that a set schedule, such as the first Thursday of every month at 8 P.M., is not viable. Although you may lose the continuity that goes along with meetings scheduled at the same time every month, there may be advantages to being more flexible about meeting times. The purpose of the meeting should drive the logistics. In other words, know why you want people to come together. Then, do everything possible to make sure that the people who need to be at the meeting can be there. Success should be measured not in numbers but in members' satisfaction.

PROGRAMING FOR GROUP MEETINGS

Successful meetings take planning. It is an unwritten rule that the more people you involve, the more people you can expect to attend. Ask for input and involvement and be responsive to the ideas that others offer. Find ways to get as many people involved as possible.

Prepare an agenda so members know what to expect at the meeting. A well-organized, carefully orchestrated meeting acknowledges the many demands on us all, and people appreciate the effort. Good planners don't waste anybody's time, their own or the members'. That means more than starting and finishing promptly: it means being sure to give participants something they want or need, such as information or support. There should always be time for socializing, usually at the close of the more structured portion of the meeting. The business portion is important, but should be covered quickly because the people coming together may have little time away from home and look forward to the learning and sharing. An agenda should be included with the meeting announcement and sent at least two weeks before the meeting. People need adequate time to decide if they wish to attend and to make the necessary arrangements. If the announcement is sent too far in advance, however, people may forget. Always include in the meeting announcement the name and telephone number of a contact person who can be called for more information. Members should be urged to check with the contact person in case of bad weather to find out if the meeting has been canceled.

The planning committee should survey members to determine what interests them most. Topics might include advances in genetic treatment or progress in finding the gene for your disorder. If members appear to be more interested in psychosocial issues, consider speakers who can discuss ways of coping with the genetic disorder on a day-to-day basis. Tackle problem areas such as how to resolve school or job conflicts, how to obtain insurance, or how to communicate with caregivers. Research local resources with expertise in the identified areas. Network with other groups to find speakers who can address cross-disability issues. Physicians, genetic counselors, social workers, speech and physical therapists, psychologists, nurses, university faculty, clergy, local authors, and newspaper columnists are all potential speakers.

Brief each speaker before the meeting, particularly those not familiar with the medical and social ramifications of the genetic disorder represented by your group. Be specific as to the amount of time allotted, the content of the speech, and the audience's level of knowledge. Be sure that the speaker will allow time for questions and will stay for informal discussion during the social time at the end of the meeting. Ask how the speaker would like to be introduced, and assign someone to prepare an appropriate introduction. A volunteer should also be responsible to meet, greet, and take care of the speaker, who should be treated as a special guest from arrival to departure. Be sure to write a thank-you note after the meeting, and you will have the basis for an ongoing relationship.

Vary your programs. Invite representatives from other genetic support groups to talk about how their group functions. Show a videotape on some aspect of genetics such as the Human Genome Project (the worldwide research effort to determine the location of the estimated fifty thousand to a hundred thousand human genes), and invite an ethicist to lead a discussion about the potential issues of mapping the human genome. Focus on humor as a coping mechanism. Present a panel composed of members led by a professional skilled in group dynamics. Whatever the program, give members an opportunity to evaluate both the presenter and the content.

While people come to meetings for the program, many come to find support. They seek a sense of belonging. Make an effort to create a welcoming environment. Whether the setting is someone's living room, a borrowed office, or a social hall at the local YMCA, it is the people who make the meeting work. Establish a phone squad to call members and remind them of an upcoming meeting. Try a buddy system to encourage people to come to meetings together and to ease the entry of newcomers. Make sure everyone who wants to attend has transportation. Find out if families need child care assistance in order to attend. You may even want to create a fund to cover these costs.

Every meeting should have a chairperson who is responsible for following the agenda. As people arrive, they should be greeted by a volunteer who can answer questions and introduce newcomers to others. For smaller groups, the greeter should make sure everyone signs the attendance sheet and gets a name tag. If the number of participants is large enough to require it, set up a registration table where people can sign in and fill out name tags.

Start every meeting promptly. Some groups let each member say a few words of introduction; others introduce newcomers. Then follow the agenda, which should include specific amounts of time for each segment of the meeting. For example:

7:00–7:10	Welcome and Introductions
7:10–7:30	Business session (minutes from previous meeting, financial report, plan for needs assessment, research update)
7:30–8:00	Guest speaker
8:00–8:15	Discussion
8:15–9:00	Closing remarks (reminder of next meeting date); refreshments, socializing

Don't overlook the cost of meetings. If you don't establish a way to share expenses, the financial drain can easily become a burden. Discuss this issue with members early. Some groups simply place a bowl for donations next to the sign-in sheet. Others ask for a specific amount to cover the cost of refreshments at the end of each meeting. Some host families can absorb all costs. Professionals who provide meeting space can sometimes find money in their departmental budget. From the beginning, however, keep track of expenses. As the group grows, you will need to know the actual costs of running it.

- Form a committee to survey members about their interests and to determine the place, date, time, and content of the programs.
- Brief the speaker about time, content, and members' knowledge level. Allow time for questions. Write a thank-you note to the speaker.
- Vary the programs and the format.
- Always create a welcoming environment. Provide name tags.

- Ask for involvement from members.
- Establish a phone squad to remind members of an upcoming meeting.
- Find ways to cover the cost of the meetings.

SUPPORT SESSIONS

Groups that come together for support have special concerns. The format and content differ significantly from those of the typical membership meeting described above. For such sessions, chairs should always be arranged in a circle, of which everyone is a part. While someone needs to function as the leader or facilitator to keep the discussion moving and to stop disruptive behavior, members of the group should set the priorities and each meeting's agenda in response to the needs of the participants. The leader is not an expert. Everyone has a role to play, and rules must be agreed upon in advance for the group process to work. Here is a sampling from Greene's *Guide to Establishing HD Support Groups:*

- Speak one at a time.
- Speak in the first person.
- Do not judge others.
- Do not be defensive; accept other members' feelings.
- Be honest.
- Any topic can be raised for discussion.
- You do not have to speak, but all members are encouraged to participate.

Perhaps most basic of all is the need for confidentiality. Members need to trust each other if they are going to open up and talk honestly about personal subjects and feelings. They need to know that what they say will stay within the group. As people have different ideas of what constitutes confidentiality, the group's interpretation must be agreed upon in the beginning. Every possibility, from the rule, Nothing Leaves This Room, to asking permission before sharing information with someone outside the group, needs to be considered. In the process, some people may realize that their personal style may not fit with the group. Some people like to gossip too much. Others feel uncomfortable hearing the kinds of intimate feelings and experiences that are shared within self-help or mutual aid groups.

Concerns about confidentiality should extend to all interactions, whether they are face to face, by telephone, or even on paper. Assuming that the purpose of all group activities is to do more good than harm, leaders need to establish policies regarding the use of all information from or about affected individuals and their families. This caution applies to photographs printed in the newsletter, describing a "case" to a reporter, sharing names with researchers, or even distributing a publication that contains personal stories or letters from families to a broader audience. People's right to privacy needs to be respected, and groups must be especially careful to set a level of confidentiality that keeps the most reserved members comfortable. Professionals can be helpful in leading discussions about this critical issue and perhaps can identify more established groups that are willing to share their experiences in protecting members' privacy.

Certain skills enhance the group process. The ability to be an effective listener, for example, works in a group setting as well as in a peer support, or one-on-one, situation. Other communication skills are required to keep a group discussion flowing. A trained facilitator knows how to keep a discussion focused. There are proven techniques for moving a discussion away from inappropriate topics and for handling difficult situations. These include intervening when one individual monopolizes the group, comforting an individual overcome by emotion, and defusing conflicts that erupt between members. Many professionals have mastered these skills and are willing to share techniques with group members. Building such skills, moreover, is so relevant for personal and organizational growth that it easily can be the focus of a program or even a series of meetings.

LEGISLATION AND ADVOCACY

Although it is difficult to keep up with all the federal and state legislation that has to do with genetics, it is important to try. Group members need to know what laws and regulations are being proposed that can affect them. They also need opportunities to participate in the political process as a means of advocating for their own interests.

Though few people feel confident taking on congressional committees by themselves, most people are willing to add their voice to a collective call for change. The process works. Abbey Meyers learned her way around Washington from her mentor, the late Marjorie Guthrie: "Besides opening doors and shoving me through, Marjorie had a unique way of thinking because she was simply a housewife just like me. Once when we met with an FDA commissioner, he talked so technically that only Washington insiders could have interpreted what he was saying. 'Listen,' said Marjorie, 'I'm only a housewife. Speak to me in English so I can understand.' When I asked her why she had done that, she told me that by making the commissioner repeat and simplify what he meant, she had made him commit himself, which no government bureaucrat ordinarily does."

Small groups parlay their power by joining cross-disability coalitions, such as the Alliance of Genetic Support Groups, National Organization for Rare Disorders, and the Consortium for Citizens with Disabilities. Also, coalitions, organizations, and individuals come together through groups like Research!America and Independent Sector in a common cause.

Genetic support groups frequently encourage advocacy efforts for improved legislation that will directly affect their members. Some groups lobby at the local, state, and federal levels to introduce, change, or repeal current laws relating to the genetic disorders they represent. Others work to increase federal funding for mapping genes, finding treatments, and discovering cures for particular genetic disorders.

More and more, persons with genetic disorders are recognizing the importance of becoming involved in their own care, of exercising as much control in their lives as possible, and of influencing policy decisions that affect them and their families. For example, many provisions in the Americans with Disabilities Act address the needs of individuals in wheelchairs but do not take into consideration the accessibility of public conveniences for persons of short stature. Consequently, when the United States Architectural and Transportation Barriers Compliance Board proposed extending the height of automatic bank teller machines, Little People of America (LPA) conducted a massive letter-writing campaign urging reconsideration of the change. Through this grassroots efforts, LPA involved its more than five thousand members in advocacy that could benefit a great many other people as well.

The Immune Deficiency Foundation

NATIONAL

NEWSLETTER

Number 17/Summer 1992
*Our area code is currently being changed to 410.
If you experience any difficulty getting through, use the
301 exchange, which will remain in use until November 1992.*

P.O. BOX 586 COLUMBIA, MD 21045 (410) 461-3127 (800) 296-4433 / FAX: (410) 461-3292   *Editors: Sara LeBien, Marcia Boyle and Toni Volk*

SPECIAL EDITION

INSURANCE REIMBURSEMENT ISSUES

President's Message

Access to good affordable health care through adequate health insurance has become an increasingly urgent issue for patients and families concerned with primary immune deficiency. Unfortunately, we are dealing with disorders that involve both a preexisting condition and chronic and often expensive therapy. Given the present state of health insurance in this country, that leaves our population extremely vulnerable.

The Immune Deficiency Foundation has worked in the past and is increasing its efforts for the future to serve as a resource for patients and families concerned with health insurance. One step we have taken is to produce this issue of the IDF NEWSLETTER which examines different problems of health care coverage and options available to patients and families. We are grateful to the efforts of Sara LeBien, Ruth Pritchard and the insurance representatives of companies which produce products and services used by our patient population for the compiling and writing of the articles presented in the Newsletter.

The committee of experts which we assembled to produce this issue will continue to work with IDF to keep the patient population abreast of health insurance information in future

issues. In addition, we have taken the steps to better train our staff and chapter representatives to serve as patient advocates on health insurance. The article entitled, *"IDF Insurance And Reimbursement Workshop,"* describes the recent health insurance workshop sponsored for IDF and the role which the Foundation representatives can play in assisting patients and families. In addition, the second edition of the IDF PATIENT AND FAMILY HANDBOOK, which will be available early in 1993, will contain a new and expanded section on health insurance.

We welcome your questions, but we would welcome your help even more. Our chapters and support groups need people who are committed to joining together to make a difference in their local areas. Locally and nationally we can work together for insurance reform if we have enough people who are willing to help. The IDF needs your involvement and support to continue its efforts to focus attention on issues such as health insurance which affect the patients, families and medical professionals we represent.

Marcia Boyle

Newsletters can be effective as a medium for addressing relevant issues. (Immune Deficiency Foundation)

No one questions that there is power in numbers. However, advocacy can be a powerful tool in the hands of passionate individuals. Groups with small numbers can take their message to decision makers by writing letters, giving testimony, and educating anyone who will listen. As a result of an intensive campaign by a handful of committed families from the Dystrophic Epidermolysis

Bullosa Research Association of America, for example, Congress allocated $5 million for research to cure this devastating genetic skin disease.

Lobbying in the public interest is allowed and even encouraged. Organizations that are incorporated under Section 501(c)(3) of the Internal Revenue Code, however, have certain limitations as a result of their nonprofit status. According to a readable pamphlet on this subject by Independent Sector (1994, p. 1), charities are required by law to be nonpartisan: "Public charities can neither endorse political candidates themselves nor mobilize constituents to support or defeat candidates. Nor can they otherwise take sides in election campaigns. They can't align themselves with political parties. They can't make financial contributions to political candidates nor to candidates' or parties' campaign treasuries. And since they can't contribute, of course, they can't threaten to withhold contributions. Thus when charities lobby, they can only speak to the issues."

There are legal limits to the amount of money a nonprofit organization can spend on lobbying activities without being taxed. To complicate matters, the rules and regulations are complex, and it is difficult to get agreement on what constitutes lobbying. In other words, when is educating really lobbying? Furthermore, charities are coming under increased scrutiny, and legislation is frequently being proposed that could significantly curtail lobbying by nonprofits. Groups are advised to consult professionals with expertise in the area of nonprofit accounting to protect their 501(c)(3) status.

PARTICIPATING IN RESEARCH

For some groups, support for research is a top priority. Others may allocate their financial resources to the delivery of direct services to patients and families or to educational efforts. Everyone, however, is affected by breakthroughs in the laboratory, whether they advance the understanding of a genetic disorder or lead to better treatments or a cure. Even though leaders are not expected to be scientific experts, members do want to be kept current about their own disorder and about such developments as gene mapping and gene therapy. Technological advances in testing, prenatal diagnosis, and in vitro fertilization techniques offer exciting new possibilities for couples at risk for genetic disorders. They also raise profound questions about human responsibility and the unlimited uses of biotechnology. Your

QUESTIONS TO ASK IF YOU ARE THINKING ABOUT VOLUNTEERING FOR A RESEARCH PROJECT

General Information

What is the purpose of the study?

What are the names of the investigators?

Who would be my contact person (and what is his or her phone number)?

What agency is funding the research?

Benefits of Participating

What are the benefits of participating in this research? For myself or family members? for others?

Risks of Participating

What are the general risks of participating in this research?

What physical risks may exist?

What are some of the personal issues that could cause harm to me or my family (e.g., anxiety, stigma, discrimination, unpredicted disclosure of information)?

Treatment Issues

Will treatment be provided if unexpected problems arise while I am participating in the study?

Who will pay for this treatment?

Support and Special Services

May I bring a friend or family member to help me, either while deciding to participate or while participating?

Will special services be available for me if I need them (e.g., an interpreter, Braille, child care)?

Costs and Reimbursement

How will the costs associated with participation in this research be handled?

Is there compensation for the time involved?

Will the costs associated with travel/child care/special services be reimbursed?

What additional health care costs may be associated with participation (e.g., will hospitalization or procedures such as scans and blood tests be billed to me or to my insurance)?

Storage of Genetic Information

What will happen to the stored DNA sample or any of my genetic information after this project is completed?

What will happen if I decide to withdraw from this project?

If this research plan changes in the future, if additional steps are added, or if new findings emerge, will I be notified and asked to sign another consent form?

Will any of my genetic information be distributed (e.g., to pharmaceutical or biotechnology companies, genetic laboratories, or governmental agencies)?

Involvement of Other Family Members

What happens if I need to have other family members involved in the study? How will they be contacted and by whom?

What will happen to the cells, DNA, or personal genetic information if they choose not to participate at all or withdraw from the study?

Study Results and Confidentiality Issues

What will happen to the results of my tests from the study?

Will I receive the test results? If so, how?

May I choose not to receive the results?

Can I change my mind?

Will the results be put anywhere except in the research records?

How will the confidentiality of the records, including photographs, be maintained?

Communication and Followup

How will the results of the research project be communicated to participants?

If genetic services, tests, or treatments are developed from this research, how will I be told of their availability?

How will I be informed if you publish information about me and my family?

What happens if I do not participate in the research?

Alliance of Genetic Support Groups, 1993

medical or scientific advisors can be most helpful in keeping members up-to-date in this rapidly changing area.

In addition to knowing about current research, group members usually welcome opportunities to play a meaningful role. Under the guidelines of confidentiality, however, neither the group nor professionals should give a potential participant's name to a researcher without permission. Rather, information about the study should be widely publicized so that individuals can contact the study director personally to indicate their interest.

Before initiating outreach to members, ask the investigator for a summary statement describing the purpose of the study, its methodology, and the criteria on which the study will be evaluated. Have your medical or scientific advisors review the proposed project to determine if it is in your members' best interest. Once you are assured that all aspects of the project are acceptable, you can inform members or get permission to release their names.

There are many types of genetic research, and the role of volunteers varies. Sometimes, involvement is limited to a one-time donation of a blood sample; other times, volunteers are needed for long-term clinical studies. But in any case, it is important for groups to educate their members about informed consent: giving informed consent to participate in a research project means agreeing voluntarily to take part in the study that has been fully explained. The volunteer confirms that he or she has been given all the information necessary to make a knowledgeable decision about participating in the project. The Alliance of Genetic Support Groups has developed a list of questions to guide people who are thinking about volunteering for a research project (see pages 94–95).

Volunteers should be encouraged to read all documents very carefully before signing them. They should know that it is never too late to ask questions. In addition, a copy of any signed document should be given to the volunteer for his or her personal records.

PATIENT REGISTRIES

In 1990, when Jannine Cody started a group for families interested in conditions involving chromosome 18, her objective was to establish a registry to link researchers with patients. In a short time, she realized that for the families she had identified, the need to share information and to support each other took precedence over research. The group's name remains the Chromosome 18 Registry and Research Society, but in response to members' priorities, its mission has broadened. The registry, however, has proved to be a valuable service to members and an incentive for families to affiliate with the organization.

Patient registries like the one maintained by the Chromosome 18 Society are invaluable to researchers seeking patients with rare genetic disorders. Registries maintained by voluntary health organizations can also have other important uses. The most common purpose is to provide information and to improve access to care for patients. A special list, however, might be used to identify families willing to talk to the media or to give testimony before legislative bodies. Some registries function as a resource for matching parents for peer, or one-to-one, support. A pen pal group maintains a registry to link youngsters of the same age who have similar conditions.

The use of the information in the listing is what defines the kind of information required and distinguishes a registry from an ordinary membership list. Common to all registries, however, is the need to protect the privacy of individuals and the confidentiality of information. People rarely think of these issues when joining a group or merely communicating with an organization, so it is up to responsible leaders to establish appropriate policies governing the release of people's names as well as information about specific families or cases.

Groups should publicize such policy in materials that target the public, especially membership brochures and forms. This practice helps educate consumers by explaining why the group is requesting certain types of information and possible ways it might be used.

Looking at groups as appropriate repositories for case identification for research scientists, *Guidelines for Rare Disease Patient Registries* (Meyers and Mize, 1992) suggests information that should be requested:

- Subject's name
- Subject's address
- Subject's telephone number
- Patient's name
- Relationship of subject to patient (relative, friend, etc.)

- Patient's present age or birth date
- Patient's age at the time of diagnosis
- Diagnosis or diagnoses
- Name, address, and telephone number of treating physician
- Subject's interest in research participation (yes, maybe, no)
- Permission to release subject's name to a scientific investigator

---

To be useful, this information should be entered into a secure computer database, where it can be retrieved by category. Files can be maintained by hand and kept in locked cabinets, but such a system is slow and cumbersome. Regardless of the system used, however, registry records must be managed with great care. Someone needs to be responsible for the security of the information as well as its accuracy and currency.

Persons wishing to participate in a registry must sign and date a permission form allowing the release of their name. A parent must give signed permission for a minor. These permission forms, which must also be kept on file, can be blanket or specific and must protect the group as well as the individual.

Deciding who can have access to a registry should be accomplished by a formal review process. Medical advisors can play a vital role in helping to develop the process and by participating in the evaluation of requests from researchers seeking the group's cooperation. Every proposal should describe the purpose of the study, the methodology, and criteria for evaluation. (See sample Summary of Proposal used by the Chromosome 18 Registry.) In addition to judging the merits of the study, its medical value, and its potential benefit to the group, reviewers should also consider the credentials of the research team. Only after a project is approved should the group release the names of patients who might participate.

In cases where a group has no established procedure for securing permissions or lacks sufficient data for identifying likely research subjects, the leaders may decide to assist a researcher by publicizing an approved project and letting members who are interested initiate contact themselves. Sometimes, a group will send a letter to patients informing them of a proposed (and approved) project and request that they respond directly to the researcher. In such a situation, the researcher usually pays for the mailing and supplies stamped, addressed envelopes for replies.

The Chromosome 18 Registry and Research Society developed a certificate of cooperation that researchers who were approved to work with the group must sign. The certificate emphasizes the need for confidentiality as well as for obtaining informed consent. In response to complaints that researchers rarely share the results of their work with participants, the registry has created an unusual, but appropriate, condition: "The researcher will provide the Registry and each participating family with a summary, in lay language, of the progress of the project at least once every 12 months. This information may be used to inform members of the Registry of the research activities currently ongoing. If the researcher feels the information is confidential and does not wish to make it public at that time, these wishes will be honored."

There are other ways groups can promote research through registries. For many years the Tourette Syndrome Association has supported a brain bank program. Through an extensive outreach program, the association educates patients, possible carriers, and the public about the need for human brain tissue for research into the cause of this little-understood syndrome. The association assumes all costs directly related to obtaining tissue from a donor registered in the program, and assistance is available twenty-four hours a day from brain banks on the East and West Coasts to ensure the proper handling of the much-needed tissue. Groups concerned with other neurological disorders (such as Huntington disease, Rett syndrome, and dystonia) collaborate with the brain banks, physicians, and pathologists to ensure that researchers have sufficient tissue for their projects.

The Chromosome 18 Registry and Research Society

6302 Fox Head • San Antonio, TX 78247 • (210) 657–4968

Summary of Proposal

1. Title of Research Proposal _____

2. Principal investigator _____
   Associate investigators _____

3. Mailing address _____

4. Phone number ( ) _____ Fax number ( ) _____

5. Anticipated starting date of project _____

6. Anticipated length of project _____

7. Which group of families are you asking for access to (18q–, 18p–, etc.)? _____

8. Number of families (patients) need to participate _____

9. What will you be asking families to do? _____

10. Funding source _____

11. Attach a copy of your Institutional Review Board (IRB) approval letter. (IRB approval is required. If IRB is concerned about availability of patients, the Registry will provide information relating to the number of potential patients which would be available for the proposal to help in their decision.)

12. Please attach a short summary of the proposal which is not more than one double-spaced page in length.

13. Please submit a copy of the entire research proposal including a copy of the informed consent document.

Documents used by the Chromosome 18 Registry and Research Society to review research proposals and spell out researchers' responsibilities with regard to protecting privacy. (Chromosome 18 Registry and Research Society)

The Chromosome 18 Registry and Research Society

6302 Fox Head • San Antonio, TX 78247 • (210) 657–4968

Certificate of Cooperation

If the project is accepted by the Registry's Board of Directors, the researcher will agree to the following conditions:

1. The researcher will not release any personal identification information about anyone who has contacted them about participating in their research due to their membership in the Registry. The only exception being to the family's health care provider or the Registry.

2. The researcher will not distribute any blood, tissue, cell lines or any patient medical information derived from Registry families to any other investigator if they are accompanied by any personal identification information. If a researcher does wish to distribute such samples with personal identification information, neither the samples or information may be sent until the recipient researcher has obtained approval from the Registry and informed consent from each family involved.

3. The researcher will provide the Registry and each participating family with a summary, in lay language, of the progress of the project at least once every 12 months. This information may be used to inform members of the Registry of the research activities currently ongoing. If the researcher feels the information is confidential and does not wish to make it public at that time, their wishes will be honored.

4. The researcher will report to the Registry the names of each new family that has decided to participage in their project in the past 60 days. This will help us to facilitate enrolleement in each study.

5. The Chromosome 18 Registry and Research Society will be acknowledged in any publication or presentation of data derived from our members' participation.

I _____ (principal investigator) agree to comply with the above conditions regarding any research which utilizes patients which were identified due to their membership in The Chromosome 18 Registry and Research Society. I also certify that all associate investigators will honor this agreement.

Signature _____   Date _____

All submissions must be sent to the Registry office in quadruplicate. The board will meet to review the proposal within 30 days of receipt. After approval of a project, the Registry will forward letters from the researchers to the appropriate families. Compliance with this document does not replace individual informed consent requirements.

—7—

Fund-Raising

There is money out there, and there is money for your program. You have to do your homework, and there is no way around it. But when you do, the results are well worth it.

S. STAHL
"Funding the Impossible Dream"

In the beginning, most people are more concerned with raising consciousness than with raising funds. They use their own money to buy stamps or to pay for telephone calls. It is not long before expenses begin to mount, however, and the need to identify sources of financial support gets added to the expanding "to do" list.

Early on, new groups should secure nonprofit status, which helps establish credibility and ensures that contributions are tax deductible to the extent allowed by law. The group will also be eligible for governmental and foundation funding. The process is time-consuming and can be accomplished more easily with assistance from an accountant or a lawyer experienced in dealing with the Internal Revenue Service.

To qualify, an organization must be operated for charitable, educational, or other specified exempt purposes. Except for lobbying, most of the activities of genetic support groups qualify. An applicant must provide supportive documentation, including articles of incorporation, by-laws, current financial statements, and a proposed budget for the first two years of operation. The IRS also requires details on activities conducted and planned, along with information about the group's officers. Rulings are usually made within four months of submission and are retroactive to the date the group was formed if the submission was within fifteen months of formation (Kurlander, 1992).

SAMPLE OPERATING BUDGET FOR A GENETIC
SUPPORT GROUP (in dollars)

Item	1994 Budget	1994 Actual
Income		
Dues		
Corporate	4,000	3,250
Individual	2,500	2,100
Fund-raisers		
Gift wrap sales	600	800
Direct mail appeal	1,100	1,200
Tributes	650	500
Interest	400	400
Contributions in kind	600	600
Miscellaneous	75	110
Total	9,925	8,960
Expenses		
Fund-raising		
Gift wrap sales	300	450
Direct mail appeal	700	700
Tributes	150	100
Telephone	1,600	1,850
Postage	1,000	1,100
Printing/copying	1,900	1,850
Newsletter	600	600
Meetings	750	750
Supplies	400	500
Professional fees	800	950
Miscellaneous	100	225
Total	8,300	9,075
Surplus (Loss)	1,625	(115)

Be sure to involve an accountant knowledgeable about tax laws covering nonprofit groups in all aspects of fund-raising, so that the nonprofit status is never jeopardized. It is the responsibility of the group's leaders, however, to be aware of and to understand federal and state regulations that govern tax-deductible giving, so donors get the full benefit of their charitable donation.

MEMBERSHIP DUES

Membership dues can be a constant source of funds to pay for operating costs, but keep in mind that many members may have substantial medical expenses. Furthermore, many genetic support groups are organized to help people with rare diseases, so they don't have a large base from which to draw. Consequently, new groups typically try to keep dues low to encourage and enable people to join. Though dues can be as little as $5 a year, most groups charge $25 for a family membership and establish a policy that allows the waiving of fees on a case-by-case basis. Some groups create membership categories and encourage those who can pay more to do so. In addition, those members who can are expected to donate services and time in addition to financially supporting organizational activities, such as candy sales, auctions, or raffles. Therefore, it is important to look elsewhere for the funds to support programs that benefit the members.

FUND-RAISING STRATEGIES

Most people perceive fund-raising as a necessary evil. They are willing to do almost anything except ask for money. As with most things that people don't like to do, fund-raising is easily put off. Responsible groups, however, know how much money they will need for programs and services and plan how they will obtain the necessary funds before they commit to spending it.

Try looking at fund-raising from a different perspective. As groups evolve, expenses will increase, and raising money must become a priority if a group expects to survive. In the beginning, friends and family will give money just because they are asked. They know the person asking and want to help. They trust that the money will be used properly to advance the cause. These people constitute an initial funding base. They also prove the axiom, People give to people. They prove that to get, you have to ask.

Begin keeping precise records upon receipt of the first donation. Donations should be acknowledged in writing. In addition to saying thank you, provide a receipt indicating what portion of the donation is tax deductible. These records form the basis of a sound fund-raising program. Those who have given once are the most likely to

Go public to acknowledge contributors, big and small. (Foundation for Nager and Miller Syndromes)

give again. Communicate with these supporters on a regular basis. Keep them informed, keep them involved, and they will keep giving. Ask everyone. Don't be afraid. If a person won't give money, ask for goods or services. Involve givers in the process by asking them to ask others or to open the door to potential donors. Don't take a refusal personally. There is tremendous competition for funds. Not everyone has personal involvement or even cares about your particular disorder. Even those who do, may disagree with the group's priorities: some people prefer to fund research; others want to support public education, conferences, or family services.

Please Join Us for a garden party/fundraiser for NTSAD on the occasion of Jason's attaining the age of Bar-Mitzva. We wish to share a special afternoon of live music, food and good company.

DATE: Saturday, September 24, 1994
TIME: 3pm - 7pm
PLACE: The Yard at 22 Sherburne Road, Lexington, MA
HOSTS: Karen and Jeffrey Arbetter

Response requested by September 12, 1994, Response Card on back.
Suggested gift; $36.00 per person to:

NTSAD
c/o Jason's Bar-Mitzva fundraiser
2001 Beacon Street
Brookline, MA 02146

It Is Said the greatest Mitzva ("good deed") is to inspire others to perform good deeds. On this day we wish to honor Jason whose indomitable spirit has inspired the fundraiser and the good deed associated with it.

❧ ❧ ❧

▪ *NTSAD* (National Tay-Sachs & Allied Disease) is a private non-profit health organization dedicated to the prevention and ultimate eradication of Tay-Sachs and 40 related genetic disorders.

▪ *NTSAD* programs include Education programs, Laboratory Quality Control, Tay-Sachs carrier screening, Family Support Services, Advocacy and Research.

▪ *NTSAD* has greatly enhanced our lives and the lives of families like us. We feel it is very important to support its work.

Karen + Jeffrey

Please reply by September 12, 1994. No tickets will be mailed. A guest list will be held at the gate.

Please make checks payable to NTSAD c/o Jason's Bar-Mitzva fundraiser. Contributions are tax-deductable to the extent provided by law.

The printing of this invitation has been underwritten by the generosity of Lexington Savings Bank. Many other groups and individuals have made Jason's fundraiser possible. We deeply appreciate your support.

❑ I will attend, please make _____ reservation (s) at suggested $36 each.
A check for $ _____ is enclosed.

❑ I am unable to attend. Enclosed is my donation of _____ $36 _____ $50 _____ $100 _____ other

Name _____

Address and Phone # _____

_____

IN CELEBRATION OF

JASON
AT AGE THIRTEEN

One family found a special way to honor their thirteen-year-old son, whose genetic disorder prevented his participating in a religious ceremony that marks the end of childhood. They involved family and friends in their own celebration and raised funds for their genetic support group at the same time. (National Tay-Sachs and Allied Diseases Association)

The best way to start fund-raising seriously is with a plan. It can be as elementary as making a list of potential donors and deciding on the best way to approach each one for a contribution. As needs grow, sources of funding will have to keep pace. The plan might expand to include different strategies at specific times during the year. For example, offer to sell cards year-round that are in honor of a special anniversary or in memory of a loved one, hold a garage sale in June, and conduct a direct mail appeal in November. The plan should contain details about each activity, including a project budget, a timetable, and staffing (volunteer or paid) requirements.

Who should raise money for a genetic support group? The group's members can try to raise funds. They are the ones who are most familiar with the needs and often are the most moving and eloquent spokespersons. However, watch out that the same members do not burn out from overexposure. Another approach is to involve a local service organization like the Kiwanis, Rotary, or Masons, which has a compatible mission. Local newspapers are a good source of ideas and leads. Frequently, civic or religious groups sponsor charitable fund-raisers for outside groups whose missions fit their fund-raising objectives.

It helps to know someone in the other organization, but what you know is as important as who you know. In other words, learn as much about an outside group as possible before asking them for assistance. If their sole mission is to help families of wounded fire fighters, they probably won't agree to raise funds to find a cure for a rare, genetic disorder. Again, rejections should not be taken personally. There are any number of reasons why people don't give to a particular cause; having different priorities is only one of them.

FUND-RAISING EVENTS

Each fund-raising event requires a plan of its own. The questions are basic: What? When? Where? Who? How? What will the activity cost? What will it bring in? A realistic budget for the event will reflect the planning process by taking into account all expected sources of income and all anticipated expenses. If the bottom line shows a profit, you can proceed, confident that all the work will be worth it in the end (Bishop, 1992).

Every fund-raiser needs a chairperson and committees with specific job descriptions that detail areas of responsibility. A key part

Help Fight

<u>THON SPECIAL EVENT</u>

(What is a Thon Special Event?)

A-thon event is when participants are recruited to perform a particular activity such as ride a bike - roller skate - walk - run - jog - swim - dance etc.

TWO WEEKS BEFORE THE EVENT

Participants recruit sponsors who are; friends, relatives, neighbors, businesses and teachers - anyone they know to pledge a certain amount of money based on their performance in a particular event. As participants recruit sponsors, they fill out the sponsor's name on a sponsor form along with the amount the sponsor is pledging for the participant's performance.

For example: A bike-a-thon is being held in Smithville with 35 riders -

* sponsors average pledge is .25¢ per mile -
* riders average mile is 20
* average number of sponsors per rider is 20

.25¢ x's 20 miles = $5.00 x's 20 sponsors per rider = $100.00
$100 x's 35 participants = $3,500.00.

Sometimes a sponsor would prefer to pledge a fixed amount rather than pledge an amount based on the participant's actual performance. This is acceptable.

THE DAY OF THE EVENT

After the event is completed, participants have their performance verified (number of miles ridden, walked, jogged etc.) by an official of the event. They leave one copy of the sponsor form with the official and use the other verified copy to go back and collect pledges from their sponsors.

Fund raisers should be fun as well as profitable. If people can raise money for a worthy cause while participating in an activity they enjoy, such as biking or running, everybody benefits. (Alliance of Genetic Support Groups)

of the plan is the setting of deadlines for the completion of specific tasks. Just enough meetings should be held to ensure that plans are proceeding on schedule.

Perhaps the most important decision that the group can make is the choice of the fund-raising event. Every group, whether new or

Pay Taxes by April 15th

Count Your Blessings Tax
Since taxes seem to be the style
We've come up with a little dilly —
We'll make some dough,
You'll have some fun
For our tax is really silly.
So figure up the things you can
and gladly pay your fee.
You'll see that we are taxing
Your DEAREST property.
And when the tax is finished, and
You know just what you owe,
Send the form right back to us
And don't forget the dough!

ITEM	TAX	AMOUNT DUE
I live in a house or an apartment	.50	_____
I live in a co-op or condo	1.00	_____
I have ___ TV sets	.50 each	_____
I have ___ stereos	.50 each	_____
I have ___ radios	.50 each	_____
I have ___ automobiles	.50 each	_____
I have ___ air conditioners	.50 each	_____
I have ___ electric blankets	.50 each	_____
I have ___ ceiling fans	.50 each	_____
I have ___ pets	.50 each	_____
My address has ___ numbers	.50 each	_____
My family consists of:		
Mother	1.00	_____
Father	1.00	_____
Husband/Wife	2.00	_____
Sisters/Brothers	.50 each	_____
Children	1.00 each	_____
Grandchildren	2.00 each	_____
Greatgrandchildren	3.00 each	_____
I own a VCR	1.00 each	_____
I own a Camcorder	1.00	_____
I own a personal computer	1.00	_____
I own ___ cameras	.50 each	_____
	TOTAL DUE:	$_____

Count up your blessings and mail this tax return with your check payable to:

National Tay-Sachs and Allied Diseases Association, NY Chapter
92 Washington Avenue, Cedarhurst, NY 11516

This tax bill is an example of an inexpensive fund raiser that does not even require a committee to be successful. (National Tay-Sachs and Allied Diseases Association, N.Y. Chapter) old, large or small, is limited to those activities their active volunteers are willing to support. An annual telethon, for example, requires volunteers who are willing to solicit donations over the phone. To be successful, moreover, the group must have a substantial list of previous and potential donors for them to call as well as a facility with enough telephones to get the job done in a concentrated period of time. Organizing a luncheon and fashion show or a testimonial dinner honoring a local personality requires more resources than most new groups have, particularly because such events require a great deal of volunteer time as well as a great many attendees.

New groups and small groups should concentrate on fundraisers that are not costly to run and do not require much people power. Try to be adopted by a local scout troop or youth group and to be the recipient of all funds raised when they have a car wash or bake sale. Arrange for a bookstore or restaurant to donate a percentage of their profits for a particular day or week. Have a no-show ball and suggest that people stay home and send in donations equal to the cost of a fancy evening out. Larger groups with a core of experienced workers and an established donor base are in a better position to undertake more involved activities, like an ad calendar, a cookbook, or a travel auction. Groups should encourage supporters to determine if their employers match employee gifts or make cash donations to organizations where their employees volunteer.

MATERIALS AND PUBLICITY

The development of appropriate fund-raising materials is a critical part of any good fund-raising plan. Printed pieces can help tell the group's story in a compelling way and support any personal outreach made by volunteers. Prepare a packet that explains about the organization and what it does. Establish the group's credentials. Describe the disorder represented. List the board of directors and the professional advisory board. Give a history of the organization and a brief description of its current programs and services. If you are raising funds for research, provide a description of the projects, including a profile of the leading researchers. Include reprints of human interest stories about the group or its members. Let the packet help make the case for why this specific group deserves support. Remember, people don't want to give money to a group that may disappear, and they want assurance that the money they give will be well spent.

Organize your fund-raising materials into an attractive packet and send it along as background when you publicize a fund-raiser. A press release is useful for informing the public about upcoming events. Newspaper announcements can be supplemented with fliers posted in public places. Radio stations will generally air a public service announcement for a recognized nonprofit group, as long as they receive the announcement a specified time before the date of the event.

Here are just a few types of fund-raising events that need public support to succeed:

- Walk-a-thons, bike-a-thons, swim-a-thons, dance-a-thons
- Tournaments
- Concerts, lecture series
- Raffles
- Sales: greeting cards, plants, crafts, magazines, candy, gift wrap
- Auctions: art, services, travel
- Theater parties, art shows, fashion shows, house tours
- Testimonials, roasts, dinner dances

It is appropriate and smart to write a thank-you note to everyone who contributes to the success of an event in any way. The note should describe the results and let supporters know how much their efforts are appreciated. This polite gesture keeps the door open for the next approach and increases the likelihood of a positive response.

Everyone in the group can be on the lookout for fund-raising ideas that work for others. A local photographer might give a portion of the proceeds of all sittings during three weeks before Christmas. A retailer might donate a percentage of sales during a special promotion period. A youth group might give the proceeds of a car wash. College fraternities, men's clubs, and sisterhoods frequently adopt charities. Groups benefit when local companies have a volunteer program for their employees, since they often give dollars to match volunteer hours. Human resources or community affairs managers will want a brochure or brief fact sheet describing the group and its volunteer opportunities, to determine if it meets company criteria. Members should also find out if their employers have matching gift programs. If so, their donations can be doubled.

Responsible fund-raisers take time after putting the money in the bank to evaluate all aspects of the program. They learn from their mistakes and build on their successes.

SEEKING GRANTS AND MAKING PROPOSALS

As competition for funds intensifies, groups that spend time on researching potential funders will spare themselves a great deal of frustration and disappointment. According to Stanlee Stahl, an experienced fund-raiser for nonprofit agencies, "Writing a proposal is like building a house. Planning is the foundation or the basement. The stronger you make it, the better the end result will be." You must know your program, what you are asking the funder to support. Talking about sick or critically ill children and adults is not sufficient. There are too many good programs competing for the same dollars and resources. You need a blueprint for action: a parent education program, a new approach for practitioners to interface with parents.

When you are clear about your major areas of concern and can explain why your organization is the best one to do a specific project (Raff, Duffy, and Davis, 1992), you must do extensive research to find those few funders likely to be interested in supporting it. Use the Foundation Center, an independent national service organization that provides information on private philanthropic giving (see Appendix B). Many libraries, community foundations, and other nonprofit agencies are part of a Cooperating Collections Network in every state that houses core collections of Foundation Center publications, including *User Friendly Guide*, *Foundation Fundamentals*, and *National Directory of Corporate Giving*. Use these resources to find foundations that fund your kind of program.

When you find a possible match, get the foundation's annual report. Review their previous tax returns. Call and ask for guidelines, if they have them. Read these materials very carefully. Note deadlines, requirements, and previous grant recipients. Determine the funder's major areas of interest. Some foundations do not give to single disease groups; others won't fund national organizations.

Some require audited financial statements for the past two years; others require operating budgets for the next two years. Do not waste the funder's time or your own by applying if you do not have what they want or if they do not fund what you do.

Network. Try to meet potential funders. Find out if anyone knows someone on a foundation's board. Look for opportunities to meet foundation people at conferences run by the National Society for Fund Raising Executives or local community foundations. While it does not ensure success, who you know can definitely be useful in the grant process.

Once you have researched possible funders and identified a likely match, you are ready a write a proposal. Successful grant writers know that having a good cause is not enough. When competing for funds, you must have a well-defined program with measurable results that fits the funder's priorities. Then you must be able to translate your need for money into a compelling proposal, which should include several distinct sections: a problem statement, goals and objectives, methodology, evaluation, personnel, and budget. Each of these sections requires specific information that will help build your case. Taken altogether, they should demonstrate that there is a specific problem that your group has the expertise to address. Since most funders prefer to give money to organizations with a proven track record, however, it takes a powerful proposal and probably a lucky combination of other factors for a new group to get funded.

Beginners should take courses. Community colleges and adult education programs frequently offer sessions on grant writing. Another excellent resource is the Support Center, a Washington-based nonprofit organization with offices in thirty states. Among the many inexpensive training and technical programs they offer are proposal-writing courses.

There is no better teacher than experience, and to get that experience you actually have to write a grant proposal. It is time consuming, even overwhelming, but once you conquer the process, you will understand what constitutes a good program. Once you develop a good program, finding a funder will be the easy part.

Epilogue

There is a place beyond pain and suffering that everyone instinctively strives to reach. Many roads lead there, but each must find his or her own way. Laughter makes that journey bearable and should be given along with other protective shots in childhood. In fact, professionals are beginning to promote humor as a coping technique. Julie Kurnitz, an actress who has Marfan syndrome, travels across the country with a humorous, uplifting message for support groups. She believes that we can acknowledge the seriousness of a condition without always being serious.

Julie discourages the use of words like *victim, sufferer, afflicted, tragic,* and *heartbreaking.* These, she says, are opinions, not facts. She has incorporated the philosophy into her own life, and she believes that the way we look at a disease or condition—our attitude—plays a big part in how we deal with it. The facts do not change, but we can.

A positive attitude reflects a coming to terms with life, and like the body and the spirit, a positive attitude must be cared for and fed. Passionate volunteers, some of whom have been described in this book and some of whom are reading it, once in a while need to get away from daily stressors, be they the demands of illness, family, or volunteer work. They need to distance themselves from their intense work, which can easily become all consuming. Such distancing actually can become a matter of survival.

It is important to take time for one's self: to read a book, see a movie, listen to music, exercise, or just relax. Other people can be a powerful stimulus to learning and sharpening skills. Meeting different kinds of people with a variety of interests can open up new territory to explore. Conferences and national meetings are a fertile breeding ground for new approaches to the same old problems.

Perhaps most obvious of all, it is a good idea to stop and take stock of the good things that happen in a day. The list can range from finding matching socks to having the sun shine on the weekend. Looking for the brightness feeds a positive attitude and helps many people maintain a healthy, balanced perspective.

Survivors are people who know how to be nice to themselves. They are not afraid to ask for help. They let other people give them support. They know how to listen to others, but they don't lose touch with their own feelings and needs in the process. They love themselves and, therefore, have an abundance of love to give to others. They can always find some reason to smile, and inevitably those around them tend to smile too. The result is that everyone feels better and has the strength and the motivation to do whatever needs to be done to keep feeling good.

List of Known Genetic Voluntary Organizations

Genetic voluntary organizations may last many, many years, or they may disappear from the scene after a short period of time. In any case, the contact persons may change in a year or two, necessitating a change of address and telephone number. We have listed below the names of known national genetic voluntary organizations, but we recommend that you contact the Alliance of Genetic Support Groups for updated information, including names of new groups, or for the most recent *Directory of National Genetic Voluntary Organizations and Related Resources* ($22). You can reach the Alliance at

35 Wisconsin Circle, Suite 440
Chevy Chase, MD 20815-7015
(800) 336-GENE or (301) 652-5553

Aarskog Syndrome Parents Support Group
Abiding Hearts
About Aperts
About Face U.S.A.
ACC Network (Agenesis of the Corpus Callosum)
Acoustic Neuroma Association
AHEPA Cooley's Anemia Organization
Aicardi Syndrome Newsletter, Inc.
Alagille Syndrome Alliance
Alpha 1 National Association
Alzheimer's Association
Ambiguous Genitalia Support Network
American Behcet's Association
American Juvenile Arthritis Organization

American Porphyria Foundation
American Pseudo-obstruction and Hirschsprung's Disease Society
American Sickle Cell Anemia Association
American Syringomyelia Alliance Project, Inc.
Amyotrophic Lateral Sclerosis Association
Angelman Syndrome Foundation, Inc.
Aperts Syndrome Pen Pals
ARC
Arnold-Chiari Family Network
Arthrogryposis Group
Association for Children with Down Syndrome
Association for Children with Russell-Silver Syndrome
Association for Glycogen Storage Disease
Association for Macular Diseases
Association of Birth Defect Children, Inc.
Association of Neuro-Metabolic Disorders
A. T. Children's Project (Ataxia Talangiectasia)
Attention Deficit Disorder Association
Autism Society of America
AVENUES, National Support Group for Arthrogryposis

Battens Disease Support and Research Association
Beckwith-Wiedemann Support Network
Billy Barty Foundation, Inc.

Candlelighters Childhood Cancer Foundation
Carbohydrate Deficient Glycoprotein Syndrome
CardioFacioCutaneous Support Network
Celiac Sprue Association
Center for Birth Defects Information Services, Inc.
Center for Children with Chronic Illness and Disabilities
Center for Loss in Multiple Birth
Charcot-Marie-Tooth Association
CHARGE Syndrome Foundation
Cherub, Inc. (limb disorders)
Children, Adults, Attention Deficit Disorder (CHADD)
Children's Craniofacial Association
Children's PKU Network
Chromosome Deletion Outreach, Inc.
Chromosome 18 Registry and Research Society
Chronic Granulomatous Disease Association
Cleft Palate Foundation
Coalition for Heritable Disorders of Connective Tissues

Coffin-Lowry Syndrome Foundation
Congenital Heart Anomalies—Support, Education, and Resources, Inc.
   (CHASER)
Congenital Lactic Acidosis Support Group
Cooley's Anemia Foundation, Inc.
Cornelia de Lange Syndrome Foundation
Corporation for Menke's Disease
Craniofacial Foundation of America
Crohn's and Colitis Foundation of America, Inc.
Cystic Fibrosis Foundation
Cystinosis Foundation, Inc.
Cystinuria Support Network

Dandy Walker Syndrome Support Group
Depression and Related Affected Disorders Association
Direct Link for the Disabled, Inc.
Donald J. Allen Memorial Huntington's Disease Clinic Association
Dubowitz Syndrome Parent Support Network
Dysautonomia Foundation, Inc.
Dystonia Medical Research Foundation
Dystrophic Epidermolysis Bullosa Research Association of America, Inc.

Ehlers-Danlos National Foundation
8p Duplication Support Group
Epilepsy Foundation of America

FACES, National Association for the Craniofacially Handicapped
FacioScapuloHumeral Society, Inc.
Familial Gastrointestinal Registry
Families of Children under Stress
Families of Spinal Muscular Atrophy
Families with Moyamoya Support Network
Family Empowerment Network: Support for Families Affected with
   FAS/FAE
Family Resource Center on Disabilities
Family Support Network of North Carolina
Family Voices
Fanconi Anemia Research Fund, Inc.
Fetal Alcohol Network
5P-Society
Foundation Fighting Blindness
Foundation for Ichthyosis & Related Skin Types

Foundation for Nager and Miller Syndromes
FRAXA Research Foundation, Inc. (Fragile X Syndrome)
Freeman-Sheldon Parent Support Group

Genesis Fund
Genetic Interest Group
Gilda Radner Familial Ovarian Cancer Registry
Gluten Intolerance Groups of North America
Goldenhar Syndrome Research and Information Fund

Healthy Mothers, Healthy Babies
Hear Now
Help for Incontinent People
Hemifacial Microsomia/Goldenhar Syndrome Family Support Network
Hemochromatosis Foundation, Inc.
Hereditary Disease Foundation
Hereditary Hearing Impairment Resource Registry
Hermansky-Pudlak Syndrome Network
HHT Foundation International, Inc. (Hereditary Hemorrhagic
    Telangiactasia)
Human Growth Foundation
Huntington's Disease Society of America
Hydrocephalus Association
Hydrocephalus News & Notes
Hydrocephalus Research Foundation
Hydrocephalus Support Group, Inc.

Immune Deficiency Foundation
Information and Support for DiGeorge and Shprintzen Syndrome Families
International Children's Anophthalmia Network (ICAN)
International Foundation for Genetic Research
International Joseph's Disease Foundation, Inc.
International Patient Advocacy Association
International Progeria Registry
International Rett Syndrome Association
Intestinal Multiple Polyposis and Colorectal Cancer (IMPACC)
Inverted Duplication Exchange and Advocacy
IP Support Network (Incontinentia Pigmenti)
Iron Overload Diseases Association, Inc.

Jeunes Family Support Group
Joubert Syndrome Parents-in-Touch Network, Corporation (JSPITN)

Juvenile Diabetes Foundation

Klinefelter Syndrome and Associates, Inc.
Klinefelter's Syndrome Association, Inc.
Klippel-Trenaunay Support Group

Late Onset Tay-Sachs Foundation
Laurence Moon Bardet Biedl Syndrome Network
Learning Disabilities Association of America
Lesch-Nyhan Registry
Let's Face It, Inc.
Lissencephaly Network, Inc.
Little People of America, Inc.
Lowe's Syndrome Association, Inc.
Lupus Foundation of America, Inc.

Macular Degeneration International
MAGIC Foundation for Children's Growth
Malignant Hyperthermia Association of the United States
Maple Syrup Urine Disease Family Support Group
MCAD Family Support Group
Meniere's Network
Metabolic Information Network
MHE Family Support Group (Multiple Hereditary Exostoses)
ML 4 Foundation
Moebius Syndrome Foundation
Muscular Dystrophy Association
Myasthenia Gravis Foundation of America, Inc.

National Adrenal Diseases Foundation
National Alliance for the Mentally Ill
National Alopecia Areata Foundation
National Association for Parents of the Visually Impaired
National Association for Pseudoxanthoma Elasticum
National Ataxia Foundation
National Breast Cancer Coalition
National Center for Chromosome Inversions
National Depressive and Manic-Depressive Association
National Down Syndrome Congress
National Down Syndrome Society
National Foundation for Ectodermal Dysplasias
National Foundation for Jewish Genetic Diseases, Inc.
National Fragile X Foundation

National Gaucher Foundation
National Hemophilia Foundation
National Incontinentia Pigmenti Foundation
National Leigh's Disease Foundation
National Lymphedema Network
National Marfan Foundation
National MPS Society, Inc.
National Neurofibromatosis Foundation, Inc.
National Organization for Albinism and Hypopigmentation
National Organization for Rare Disorders
National Organization on Fetal Alcohol Syndrome
National Parent-to-Parent Network
National Prune Belly Syndrome
National Psoriasis Foundation
National Scoliosis Foundation
National Sjogren's Syndrome Association
National Tay-Sachs & Allied Diseases Association, Inc.
National Tuberous Sclerosis Association, Inc.
National Urea Cycle Disorders Foundation
National Vascular Malformations Foundation
National Vitiligo Foundation, Inc.
Neurofibromatosis, Inc.
Nevoid Basal Cell Carcinoma Syndrome Support Group
(New England) Retinoblastoma Support Group
NF-2 Sharing Network

Ollier's Disease Self-Help Group
Organic Acidemia Association
Osteogenesis Imperfecta Foundation, Inc.
Oxalosis and Hyperoxaluria Foundation

Pallister-Hall Foundation
Pallister-Killian Family Support Group
Parent Assistance Committee on Down Syndrome
Parents and Researchers Interested in Smith-Magenis Syndrome (PRISMS)
Parents of Galactosemic Children
Polycystic Kidney Research Foundation
Prader-Willi Syndrome Association (USA)
Purine Research Society

Research Trust for Metabolic Diseases in Children
Restless Legs Syndrome Foundation, Inc.
Retinoblastoma Support Group (New England)

Rubinstein-Taybi Parent Group

Scapuloperoneal Disease Association
Scleroderma Federation
Share and Care Cockayne Syndrome Network
Shy-Drager Syndrome Support Group
Sjogren's Syndrome Foundation, Inc.
Smith-Lemli-Opitz Advocacy & Exchange
Sotos Syndrome Support Association
Spina Bifida Association of America
Spondylitis Association of America
Sturge-Weber Foundation
Sudden Arrhythmia Death Syndrome Foundation
Support and Education Network for FAS Parents and Caregivers
Support and Educational Exchange for Klinefelter's Syndrome, Inc.
Support Group for Monosomy 9p
Support Organization for Trisomy 18, 13, and Related Disorders

Thalassemia Action Group
Thrombocytopenia Absent Radius Syndrome Association (TARSA)
Tourette Syndrome Association, Inc.
Treacher Collins Foundation
Turner's Syndrome Society of the United States

United Cerebral Palsy Association, Inc.
United Leukodystrophy Foundation, Inc.
United Scleroderma Foundation, Inc.
Usher Family Support

Velo-Cardio-Facial Syndrome Educational Foundation
VHL Family Alliance
Von Hippel-Lindau Syndrome Foundation, Inc.

Williams Syndrome Association
Wilson's Disease Association
Wolf-Hirshhorn (4p-) Parent Contact Group

X-Linked Myotubular Myopathy Resource Group

Resources

Alliance of Genetic Support Groups
35 Wisconsin Circle, Suite 440
Chevy Chase, MD 20815-7015
(800) 336-GENE or (301) 652-5553

National coalition of voluntary genetic organizations, consumers, and professionals, funded in part by the Genetic Services Branch of the Maternal and Child Health Bureau, linking individuals and families to appropriate genetic support groups and services and giving voice to those with genetic disorders. Publications include the monthly *Alert* and a *Directory of National Genetic Voluntary Organizations and Related Resources.*

Council of Regional Networks for Genetic Services (CORN)
Cynthia Hinton, MS, MPH, Coordinator
Division of Medical Genetics, Department of Pediatrics
Emory University
2040 Ridgewood Drive
Atlanta, GA 30322
(404) 727-5731

National umbrella organization, funded by the Genetics Services Branch of the Maternal and Child Health Bureau, representing the ten regional genetics networks. Composed of providers and consumers of genetics services, CORN coordinates and implements national activities in data collection, quality assurance, public and professional education, new technologies, ethical considerations, and funding for services.

Regional Genetics Networks

The United States is divided into ten regions, each of which has a genetics network representing consumers and providers of genetic services. Listed below is information about each regional genetics network that is current as of June 1995. Note: Coordinators for CORN and for the regional genetic networks change periodically. For updated information, call the Genetics Services Branch of the Maternal and Child Health Bureau at (301) 443-1080.

Genetic Network of New York State, Puerto Rico, and the
  Virgin Islands (GENES)
[New York, Puerto Rico, and the Virgin Islands]
Karen Greendale and Katharine B. Harris, Co-coordinators
Laboratory of Human Genetics, Wadsworth Center for Laboratories and
  Research
NYS Department of Health
Empire State Plaza, P.O. Box 509
Albany, NY 12202-0509
(518) 473-8036
Newsletter: *GENESIS.*

Great Lakes Regional Genetics Group (GLaRGG)
[Illinois, Indiana, Michigan, Minnesota, Ohio, Wisconsin]
Louise Elbaum, Coordinator
328 Waisman Center
1500 Highland Avenue
Madison, WI 53705-2280
(608) 265-2907
Newsletter: *GLaRGG BLuRBB.*

Great Plains Genetic Service Network (GPGSN)
[Arkansas, Iowa, Kansas, Missouri, Nebraska, Oklahoma, North Dakota,
  South Dakota]
Dolores Nesbitt, Coordinator
Division of Medical Genetics, Department of Pediatrics
University of Iowa
Iowa City, IA 52242
(319) 356-4860
Newsletter: *Genexus.*

Mid-Atlantic Regional Human Genetics Network (MARHGN)
[Delaware, District of Columbia, Maryland, New Jersey, Pennsylvania,
  Virginia, West Virginia]
Gail Chiarrello, Coordinator
260 Broad Street, Suite 1900
Philadelphia, PA 19102-3865
(215) 985-6760
Newsletter: *MARGIN.*

Mountain States Regional Genetic Services Network (MSRGSN)
[Arizona, Colorado, Montana, New Mexico, Utah, Wyoming]
Joyce Hooker, Coordinator

Medical Affairs and Special Programs, Colorado Department of
  Health
4300 Cherry Creek Drive
Denver, CO 80222
(303) 692-2423
Newsletter: *MSRGSN.*

New England Regional Genetics Group (NERGG)
[Connecticut, Maine, Massachusetts, New Hampshire, Rhode Island,
  Vermont]
Joseph Robinson, Coordinator
P.O. Box 542
Mt. Desert, ME 04660
(207) 288-2704
Newsletter: *NERGG NEWS.*

Pacific Northwest Regional Genetics Group (PacNoRGG)
[Alaska, Idaho, Oregon, Washington]
Kerry Silvey, Coordinator
901 East 18th Avenue
Eugene, OR 97403
(503) 346-2610
Newsletter: *Genetics Newsletter.*

Pacific Southwest Regional Genetics Network (PSRGN)
[California, Hawaii, Nevada]
Harriet Kuliopulos, Coordinator
State of California Department of Health Services
2151 Berkeley Way, Annex Four
Berkeley, CA 94704
(510) 540-2852
Newsletter: *Genetically Speaking.*

Southeast Regional Genetics Group (SERGG)
[Alabama, Florida, Georgia, Kentucky, Louisiana, Mississippi,
  North Carolina, South Carolina, Tennessee]
Mary Rose Lane, Coordinator
Emory University School of Medicine
2040 Ridgewood Drive
Atlanta, GA 30322
(404) 727-5844
Newsletter: *SERGG.*

Texas Genetics Network (TEXGENE)
[Texas]
Judith Livingston, Coordinator

Bureau of Women and Children, Texas Department of Health
1100 West 49th Street
Austin, TX 78756
(512) 458-7700
Newsletter: *TEXGENE.*

Other Organizations

Accountants for Public Interest
1012 14th Street, N.W., Suite 906
Washington, DC 20005
(202) 347-1668
National network of accountants who volunteer their time and expertise to nonprofit organizations that cannot afford professional accounting services.

Adopt a Special Kid—America (AASK)
2201 Broadway, Suite 702
Oakland, CA 94612
(510) 451-1748
Facilitates the adoption of children with special needs; lists adoption and referral agencies in each state.

American Self-Help Clearinghouse
Saint Clares-Riverside Medical Center
25 Pocono Road
Denville, NJ 07834
(201) 625-7101; TDD: (201) 625-9053; CompuServe 70275, 1003
Develops and maintains contacts for national self-help groups and state and local self-help clearinghouses and helps start new groups and networks. Publishes *The Self-Help Sourcebook,* provides information and referral for self-help groups, and provides consultation, materials, and networking on a nationwide basis.

Association for the Care of Children's Health (ACCH)
7910 Woodmont Avenue, Suite 300
Bethesda, MD 20814
(301) 654-6549
International nonprofit educational and advocacy organization of multidisciplinary professionals and family members promoting family-centered health care policies, programs, and practices that are responsive to the psychosocial needs of children and their families.

Association of Birth Defect Children, Inc. (ABDC)
827 Irma Avenue
Orlando, FL 32803
(800) 313-2232
Sponsors national birth defect registry and parent-matching service.

Beach Center on Families and Disability
University of Kansas Bureau of Child Research
3111 Haworth Hall
Lawrence, KS 66045
(913) 864-7600
Research and training center that focuses on families with disabilities.

Compassionate Friends
P.O. Box 3696
Oak Brook, IL 60522-3696
(708) 990-0010
Self-help organization for bereaved parents and siblings.

Direct Link for the Disabled, Inc.
P.O. Box 1036
Solvang, CA 93464
(805) 688-1603
Using computers and telephones, people in need are linked to resources nationwide on their LINKUP database.

Family Voices
P.O. Box 769
Algodones, NM 87001
(505) 867-2368
National grassroots network of families and friends speaking on behalf of children with special health care needs.

Foundation Center
79 Fifth Avenue
New York, NY 10003
(212) 620-4230
Independent national service organization established by foundations to provide an authoritative source of information on private philanthropic giving. Has reference collections in San Francisco, Washington, D.C., and Cleveland. Libraries and nonprofit information centers across the country also participate in the Cooperating Collections Network to provide fund-raising information or other funding-related technical assistance in their communities.

Independent Sector
1828 L Street, N.W.
Washington, D.C. 20036
(202) 223-8100
Nonprofit coalition of eight hundred voluntary organizational, corporate, and foundation members with national interest and impact in philanthropy and voluntary action. A national forum encouraging giving, volunteering, and not-for-profit initiative. Helped to establish the volunteer standard of 5 percent of income and five hours a week: "Give Five."

March of Dimes Birth Defects Foundation
1275 Mamaroneck Avenue
White Plains, NY 10605
(914) 428-7100
Provides information and publications pertaining to birth defects and many genetic disorders; makes referrals.

MUMS National Parent-to-Parent Network
c/o Julie Gordon, President
150 Custer Court
Green Bay, WI 54301-1243
(414) 336-5333
National parent-to-parent organization that matches parents with other parents whose children have the same or similar condition. Maintains a national database and has established several statewide MUMS groups that act as a contact for their state in helping parents find resources and support.

National Center for Education in Maternal and Child Health
2000 15th Street North, Suite 701
Arlington, VA 22201-2617
(703) 524-7802
Maintains a reference collection of Maternal and Child Health Program materials, develops publications on maternal and child health topics, and provides technical assistance in educational resource development, program planning, and topical research for the development and distribution of materials pertaining to maternal and child health issues.

National Center for Human Genome Research (NCHGR)
c/o Office of Communications, National Institutes of Health
Building 31, Room 4B09
31 Center Drive MSC 2252
Bethesda, MD 20892-2252
(301) 402-0911
Oversees comprehensive research to develop a human genetic map, to examine the ethical, legal, and social issues arising from the research, and to develop the technology that must be transferred to appropriate users in the medical community and industry.

National Center for Nonprofit Boards
2000 L Street, N.W., #411
Washington, DC 20036
(202) 452-6262
Nationwide service designed to improve the effectiveness of nonprofit organizations by strengthening their boards of directors. Offers programs and services on national, state, and local levels to nonprofit organizations.

National Center for Youth with Disabilities
University of Minnesota, Box 721
420 Delaware Street, S.E.
Minneapolis, MN 55455-0392
(800) 333-6293

Information and resource center focusing on adolescents with chronic illness and disabilities and their transition to adult life.

National Council of Nonprofit Associations
1001 Connecticut Avenue, N.W., Suite 900
Washington, DC 20036
(202) 833-5740

National coalition of state associations of nonprofit organizations. Represents more than twenty thousand nonprofit community-based organizations whose purpose is to enhance the quality of life in their communities. Quarterly publication: *State Tax Trends for Nonprofits*.

National Health Information Center (NHIC)
P.O. Box 1133
Washington, DC 20013-1133
(800) 336-4797 or (301) 565-4167

National information and referral center.

National Information Center for Children and Youth with Disabilities (NICHCY)
P.O. Box 1492
Washington, DC 20013
(800) 695-0285 or (202) 884-8200

Information and referral clearinghouse offering services to children and youth with disabilities and their families.

National Network for Mutual Help Centers, Michigan Self-Help Clearinghouse
c/o Michigan Protection and Advocacy Service, Inc.
106 W. Allegan, #210
Lansing, MI 48933-1706
(800) 777-5556 or (517) 484-7373

Association of self-help clearinghouses in the United States.

National Organization for Rare Disorders (NORD)
P.O. Box 8923
New Fairfield, CT 06812
(800) 999-NORD or (203) 746-6518

Coalition of national voluntary health agencies representing individuals with rare disorders. Provides information (including computer-accessible database through CompuServe), referral, and advocacy for orphan drugs research. Links together those with the same disorder and publishes *NORD On-Line* and *Orphan Disease Update*.

National Parent Network on Disabilities (NPND)
1600 Prince Street, #115
Alexandria, VA 22314
(703) 684-6763
National parent advocacy organization specializing in education and discrimination issues. Offers training to support parents in their efforts to improve the lives of their children.

National Rehabilitation Information Center
8455 Colesville Road, Suite 935
Silver Spring, MD 20910
(800) 346-2742
Provides general information and publications on rehabilitation.

National Society of Genetic Counselors, Inc.
233 Canterbury Drive
Wallingford, PA 19086-6617
(215) 872-7608
Professional organization for genetic counselors, providing education about the genetic counseling profession.

Sibling Information Network
62 Washington Street
Middletown, CT 06457
(203) 344-7500
National clearinghouse for information relating to brothers and sisters who have a sibling with a disability.

Sibling Support Project
Children's Hospital and Medical Center
P.O. Box 5371, CL-09
Seattle, WA 98105-0371
(206) 368-4911
Maintains a database of existing programs for siblings of children with special needs.

Support Centers of America
70 10th Street, Suite 201
San Francisco, CA 94103-1302
(415) 552-7660
Offers inexpensive workshops in many cities in the United States and printed materials for many nonprofit needs.

Other Publications

Chronicle of Philanthropy
P.O. Box 1989
Marion, OH 43306-2089
Publishes twenty-four issues a year; subscription, $67.50

Exceptional Parent magazine
209 Harvard Street, Suite 303
Brookline, MA 02146-5005
(617) 730-5800

Monthly publication for parents of children and young adults with special health care needs. Provides information for networking with other families and publishes an annual directory of national organizations, associations, products, and services.

NonProfit Times
190 Tamarack Circle
Skillman, NJ 08558
(609) 921-1251

Monthly publication. Free subscription to voluntary organizations with annual budgets under $25,000.

Overview of One Group's Success

September 29, 1994

Joan O. Weiss, MSW
Executive Director
Alliance of Genetic Support Groups
35 Wisconsin Circle, Suite 440
Chevy Chase, MD 20815

Dear Joan:

When we last spoke, you informed me that you were seeking information about how families have developed support groups. I will attempt to describe how David and I created the Fanconi Anemia Research Fund (FARF), an organization which offers family support and raises funds for scientific research. We have developed this effort over the past nine years. Initially David and I did a great deal of the work ourselves, with important help from friends. In 1991 we hired a small staff. Active families throughout the country have greatly assisted our efforts.

I hope that this information will be helpful to you. Feel free to use as much as you wish - or none at all. I could well be submitting this past your deadline. At any rate, I wish you the best of success in developing your book.

In 1983, we learned that our oldest child, Kirsten, now 21, suffers from Fanconi anemia. We were subsequently to learn that of our five children, all three girls had inherited FA. Tragically, our daughter Katie died in September, 1991 at the age of 12 from this disorder. Kirsten and her seven year old sister, Amy, are relatively stable.

We began by reading all we could find on the illness affecting our children. We learned that Fanconi anemia is an inherited autosomal recessive genetic disorder which typically results in severe bone marrow failure (acute aplastic anemia). Both parents must carry the recessive gene. Affected children usually are diagnosed between the ages of 3 and 12. They are prone to infections, bruising and bleeding episodes, and frequent hospitalizations. Patients are predisposed to leukemia and other cancers. Most do not reach adulthood.

1. Getting Started: Forming a Support Group

We felt quite isolated and alone, knowing no other family whose children shared the same disorder. Consequently, in 1985, we decided to form a Fanconi anemia support group.

We first contacted a researcher who had developed a Fanconi anemia registry, and asked her to forward a letter to all FA families in her registry. Our letter outlined our interest in starting a support group and asked people to respond if they wanted to participate. In 1985, 19 families responded to our letter. By September, 1994, 350 families from 46 states and 21 foreign countries were members of our support group.

2. Support Services Offered to Families

   a) We began by preparing a newsletter which we mail to families and interested professionals. We have just completed our 16th newsletter. This newsletter brings families up-to-date on research progress, includes letters from treating physicians on medical aspects of Fanconi anemia, and provides families a forum to communicate with one another through letters and articles they submit. The newsletter is produced semi-annually.

   b) Because of the need to keep families informed of new developments on a very regular basis, we prepare *FA Family News Bulletins* between mailings of the newsletter. The *Bulletins* include information of immediate interest to FA families, such as the availability of an experimental drug trial.

   c) We maintain regular letter and telephone contact with families in our support group.

   d) In 1993, we wrote a booklet on Fanconi anemia entitled **Fanconi Anemia: A Handbook for Families & Their Physicians**. We distribute this handbook to all FA families, their physicians (upon request) and to libraries, hospitals, genetics counselling centers, social workers and other concerned professionals who request information about Fanconi anemia.

   e) We have hosted four annual FA Family Meetings. These sessions have brought FA families together from all over the United States, Canada and a few European countries. Family members have had an opportunity to learn first-hand from treating physicians and researchers. Group counselling sessions have enabled families to share feelings and learn from others going through the same experiences.

   e) We produce and mail the *FA Family Directory* to all families in the support group. This directory lists families according to state or country of residence and alphabetically. A separate section groups all families who speak a language other than English, to facilitate communication among non-English speaking families. We also provide some information about FA patients. This resource enables families to make contact with others living near them and with families sharing a common bond.

3. Developing our Organization

In 1989, we realized we needed to become a 501(c)3 organization. Researchers were requesting grants to facilitate their work; we needed to become a legal entity to raise and distribute funds. We asked a good friend and CPA to prepare the necessary paperwork for us.

a) Becoming a 501(c)(3) organization meant forming a Board of Directors. Our Board is a diverse group of 10. A doctor, counselor, molecular biologist, three fundraisers, a Nobel Prize winner in medicine and three FA family members representing different geographical regions sit on our Board. By adding family members, we hope to increase family participation in our efforts. We will continue to make an effort to include members who have a special interest and ability in raising funds.

b) Our organization needed scientific expertise in evaluating requests for funding. We therefore developed a Scientific Review Board. We tried to find members who were extremely knowledgeable in Fanconi anemia research or related areas, and were willing to donate the necessary time to evaluate research proposals. We are constantly working to expand the number of people who sit on this Board. At least two members of this Board evaluate each grant proposal.

c) Our staff is very small. We have one full-time coordinator and another position which is shared by a social worker (our Family Support Coordinator) and administrative assistant. We try to keep overhead expenses below 10%.

d) We have made many efforts to increase the visibility of our organization, and expand the numbers of families in our support group.

1. Over the past three years, our organization has conducted site visits to 27 major medical centers, teaching hospitals and transplantation units. We have met with hematologists, nurses, social workers and transplantation specialists, and distributed materials about our research fund and support group.

2. Our Fund has attended three meetings of the American Society of Pediatric Hematology, Oncology (ASPHO) in Chicago, and two meetings of the American Society of Hematology (ASH). We distribute our literature and urge treating physicians to refer families to our support group.

3. We have written to hospital social workers, diagnostic laboratories and large groups of pediatric hematologists to inform them of our efforts.

4. Supporting Scientific Research

a) Since incorporation in 1989, the Fanconi Anemia Research Fund has made continual efforts to generate funds for scientific research. We have urged all affected families to write letters to friends, family and associates, requesting contributions. Families have become quite innovative in developing a wide variety of fund raising activities.   We have applied for grants, and have approached individual donors and corporations for large donations.

b) Since 1989, our Fund has given grants to fifteen (15) laboratories studying Fanconi anemia.   Many of these laboratories are attempting to isolate the FA genes.   Others are studying the function of the one gene identified to date, and the protein encoded by this gene.   Two laboratories are attempting to create a Fanconi anemia mouse model.   Others are exploring new therapies for this disorder.

c) Since 1989, we have sponsored five annual FA Scientific Symposia.   Research scientists from the United States, Canada and Europe have met to present their latest discoveries, challenge each others' findings and develop collaborative relationships.   Much scientific progress can be directly traced to these productive meetings.

d) In 1990, our Fund sponsored the development of the Fanconi Anemia Cell Repository at Oregon Health Sciences University (OHSU), Portland, Oregon. Families contribute blood and skin samples to this repository.   Researchers at OHSU send samples upon request to any researcher who is studying Fanconi anemia.

Joan, I hope that some of the above will be helpful to other parents wanting to start such an effort.   Please feel free to put others in touch with us.   Again, I wish you the best as you complete your important work.   I feel strongly that such a book will be of immense value to parents such as ourselves who are confronted with a rare disorder.   If you need any additional information, please feel free to contact me.

Sincerely,

Lynn D. Frohnmayer
Family Support Coordinator

Glossary

Alleles The alternative forms of genes which occur at the same site on a chromosome and which determine alternative forms of a trait.

Alpha-fetoprotein (AFP) A substance made by a developing fetus which can be measured in a pregnant woman's blood or amniotic fluid to see if the baby will have certain types of birth defects, such as spina bifida.

Amniocentesis The removal of a sample of amniotic fluid, the fluid surrounding the growing baby (fetus).

Autosomal dominant inheritance The pattern of inheritance in which only one mutant or abnormal gene of a pair is necessary for expression of the trait or disorder. There is a 50 percent chance of passing the gene on to a son or daughter by a parent who has the gene.

Autosomal recessive inheritance The pattern of inheritance in which two mutant or abnormal genes of a pair are necessary for the expression of the trait or disorder. When both parents carry a mutant gene, each offspring has a 25 percent chance of manifesting a particular genetic disorder caused by having received a mutant gene from each parent. Therefore, the affected person would have received one mutant gene from each parent.

Autosome Chromosomes other than the sex (X or Y) chromosomes. Humans have twenty-two pairs of autosomes, numbered 1 through 22.

Birth defect A disorder present at birth.

Carrier An individual who possesses both a normal and an abnormal gene for a given condition. Such individuals can pass on the abnormal gene but do not exhibit the condition themselves.

Carrier couple A couple each of whom have an altered gene that may be passed on to offspring.

Chromosomal disorder A condition caused by an abnormal number or structure of chromosomes.

Chromosome   The cellular structure that stores and transmits genetic information. Chromosomes are composed of genes linked together in specific arrangements. The normal number of chromosomes in humans is forty-six.

Congenital   Existing before or at birth.

Cytogenetics   A branch of genetics dealing with the study of chromosomes.

Deletion   The loss of a portion of a chromosome as a result of chromosome breakage.

DNA (Deoxyribonucleic acid)   The substance of heredity; a large molecule that carries the genetic information necessary for the replication of cells and for the production of proteins, which are essential for growth, the building of new tissue, and the repair of injured or broken-down tissue.

DNA probe   A specific sequence of single-stranded DNA used to seek out a complementary sequence in other single strands.

Dominant   *See* Autosomal dominant inheritance.

Etiology   The cause or origin of a disease.

Gene   A unit of heredity; a segment of the DNA molecule containing the code for a specific function.

Gene mapping   Determining the relative locations of different genes on chromosomes.

Gene therapy   A medical procedure that treats a disorder by replacing a faulty gene.

Genetic counseling   Communicating information about risks for inheriting a disorder or an abnormal pregnancy outcome and discussing one's chances of having children who may be affected by a genetic disorder. Genetic counseling also includes providing information that helps individuals and couples make personal decisions about having children.

Genetic engineering   Altering genetic material to study genetic processes and, potentially, to correct genetic defects.

Genotype   The full set of genes carried by an individual, including alleles that are not expressed.

Haploid cell   A cell with half the usual number of chromosomes, such as a sperm or egg cell.

Heterozygote   An individual, sometimes called a carrier, who has two different alleles of a designated locus.

Karyotype A systemized array of chromosomes from a single cell, prepared by photography, that demonstrates the number and morphology of the chromosomes.

Linkage The relationship between two genes, or between an identifiable trait and a genetic disorder. Genes that are located relatively close to each other on the same chromosome are said to be linked.

Locus The position of a gene on a chromosome.

Marker A detectable genetic variant. Some closely linked markers can be used to deduce the presence or absence of disease-producing genes.

Multifactorial Caused by many genetic and nongenetic factors.

Mutation Change in genetic material.

Pedigree A diagram showing a genetic family history and biological relationships among members of a family, often for several generations.

Phenotype The entire expressed physical and biochemical constitution of an individual, resulting from the interaction of the genetic endowment with the environment.

Polymorphism An inherited variation.

Prenatal diagnosis The testing of the genetic makeup of a fetus by amniocentesis or chorionic villus sampling (CVS).

Proband An affected individual through whom a family comes to medical attention.

Recessive *See* Autosomal recessive inheritance.

Recombinant DNA The hybrid DNA produced in the laboratory by joining pieces of DNA from different sources.

Recurrence risk The probability that a genetic disorder or birth defect that exists in a family will recur in offspring yet to be born.

Screening The testing of a large group of apparently healthy people for hidden disorders or risk of disorders.

Sex chromosomes The chromosomes (X and Y) involved in sex determination. Normal females have two X chromosomes in each cell, and normal males have one X and one Y.

Syndrome A pattern or group of malformations or symptoms due to a single cause.

Teratogen Any agent that causes congenital malformations.

Translocation The transfer of all or one part of a chromosome to another location on the same chromosome or to a different chromosome after chromosome breakage.

Trisomy   A state in which there are three members of a given chromosome instead of the normal pair.

X linked   Refers to any gene found on the X chromosome or traits determined by such genes. Refers also to the specific mode of inheritance of such genes.

References

Ablon, J. 1984. *Little People in America: The Social Dimensions of Dwarfism.* New York: Praeger.

Alliance of Genetic Support Groups. 1990. *National Conference on Peer Support Training: Program and Abstracts.* Chevy Chase, Md.: Alliance of Genetic Support Groups.

———. 1991. *Needs Assessment Survey for Genetic Support Groups.* Chevy Chase, Md.: Alliance of Genetic Support Groups.

———. 1992. *Proceedings: A National Conference on the Empty Pocket Syndrome: How to Get Funds.* Chevy Chase, Md.: Alliance of Genetic Support Groups.

———. 1993. *Informed Consent: Participation in Genetic Research Studies.* Chevy Chase, Md.: Alliance of Genetic Support Groups.

———. 1995. *Directory of National Genetic Voluntary Organizations and Related Resources.* Chevy Chase, Md.: Alliance of Genetic Support Groups.

Aylstock, M. 1994. *The Even Exchange: The Newsletter of Klinefelter Syndrome and Associates,* no. 9. Roseville, Calif.: Klinefelter Syndrome and Associates.

Barty, B. 1982. *Little People of America Souvenir Book.* Studio City, Calif.: Little People of America.

Bennett, R. L. 1990. In support of support groups: The role of genetic self-help groups in medical genetics. *Genetics Northwest* 5:3–5.

Bishop, K. K., J. Woll, and P. Arango. 1993. *Family/Professional Collaboration for Children with Special Health Needs and Their Families.* Rockville, Md.: Maternal and Child Health Bureau.

Black, R. B., and J. O. Weiss. 1988. A professional partnership with genetic support groups. *American Journal of Medical Genetics* 29:21–33.

———. 1990. Genetic support groups and social workers as partners. *Health and Social Work* 15:91–97.

Borman, L. D. 1992. Introduction: Self-help/mutual aid groups in strategies for health. In Katz et al., 1992.

Calder, A. E. 1990. People to people: National Kidney Foundation of Wisconsin. In Alliance of Genetic Support Groups, 1990.

Ciccariello, P. 1986. How to recruit, expand, and retain membership. In Weiss et al., 1986.

————. 1993. Personal communication.

Clark, T., and M. Hughes. 1992. *Sickle Cell Mutual Help Groups: African Americans Supporting One Another.* Chapel Hill: Psychological Research Division, University of North Carolina.

Finucane, B., A. McCoonkie-Rosell, and A. Cronister. 1993. *Fragile X Syndrome: A Handbook for Families and Professionals.* Elwyn, Penn.: Elwyn, Inc.

Forts, A. M. 1994. Up syndrome brings friends. *News 'n Views* 1(1):11–12. New York City: National Down Syndrome Society.

Greene, R. 1992. *You Are Not Alone! A Guide to Establishing Huntington's Disease Support Groups.* New York: Huntington's Disease Society of America.

Guthrie, M. 1979. A personal view of genetic counseling. In Y. E. Hsia et al., eds., *Counseling in Genetics.* New York: Alan R. Liss.

Hedrick, H. L., D. H. Isenberg, and C. J. M. Martini. 1992. Self-help groups: Empowerment through policy and partnerships. In Katz et al., 1992.

Independent Sector. 1994. *Charity Lobbying and the Public Interest.* Washington, D.C.: Independent Sector.

Katz, A. H., and E. I. Bender, eds. 1990. *The Strength in Us: Self-Help Groups in the Modern World.* New York: New Viewpoints.

Katz. A. H., et al., eds. 1992. *Self-Help: Concepts and Applications.* Philadelphia: Charles Press.

Kubler-Ross, E. 1969. *On Death and Dying.* New York: Macmillan.

Kurlander, N. 1992. Nuts and bolts. In Alliance of Genetic Support Groups, 1992.

Kurtz, L. F. 1990. The self-help movement: Review of the past decade of research. *Social Work and Groups* 13:101–15.

Madara, E. 1990. Developing self-help groups: Ten suggested steps for professionals. In Madara and Meese, 1990.

Madara, E., and A. Meese. 1990. *The Self-Help Sourcebook: Finding and Forming Mutual Aid Self-Help Groups.* Denville, N.J.: American Self-Help Clearinghouse.

March of Dimes Birth Defects Foundation. 1992. *Genetic Counseling.* White Plains, N.Y.: March of Dimes Birth Defects Foundation.

Meyers, A., and S. Mize. 1992. *Guidelines for Rare Disease Patient Registries.* Rockville, Md.: Consortium on Rare Diseases (CORD).

National Tay-Sachs and Allied Diseases Association. 1994. *The Home Care Book: A Parent's Guide to Caring for Children with Progressive Neurological Diseases.* Brookline, Mass.: National Tay-Sachs and Allied Diseases Association.

Powell, T. 1987. *Self-Help Organizations and Professional Practice.* Silver Spring, Md.: NASW Press.

———. 1990. *Working with Self-Help.* Silver Spring, Md.: NASW Press.

Poyadue, F. S. 1990. Basics of a program: Training, assessing needs, setting standards. In Alliance of Genetic Support Groups, 1990.

Raff, B. S., E. A. Duffy, and J. G. Davis. 1992. Grant writing 101. In Alliance of Genetic Support Groups, 1992.

Remine, D., R. M. Rice, and J. Ross. 1984. *Self-Help Groups and Human Service Agencies: How They Work Together.* New York: Family Service America.

Santelli, B. 1990. *Parent to Parent Information Packet.* IP-1. University of Kansas: Beach Center on Families and Disability.

Saxton, M. N.d. The something that happened before I was born. In A. J. Brightman, ed., *Ordinary Moments: The Disabled Experience.* Baltimore, Md.: University Park Press.

Schild, S., and R. B. Black. 1984. *Social Work and Genetics: A Guide for Practice.* New York: Haworth.

Scott, J. A. 1988. Genetic counseling. In *Genetic Applications: A Health Perspective.* Lawrence, Kan.: Learner Managed Designs.

Silverman, P. 1992. An introduction to self-help groups. In White and Madara, 1992.

Smith, J. C. 1990. Association for children with Down syndrome: Parent peer counselor training program. In Alliance of Genetic Support Groups, 1990.

Stahl, S. 1992. Funding the impossible dream. In Alliance of Genetic Support Groups, 1992.

Stickney, H. 1990. The first contact. In Alliance of Genetic Support Groups, 1990.

Trombino, B., and B. Bernhardt. 1990. Limitations of peer support. In Alliance of Genetic Support Groups, 1990.

Vullo, R., and B. Modell. 1990. *What Is Thalassemia?* New York: Cooley's Anemia Foundation, Inc.

Weigle, L. 1986. When and how to provide referral services. In Weiss et al., 1986.

Weiss, J. O. 1989. Genetic support groups: A continuum of genetic services. *Women and Health* 15:37–53.

———. 1993. Genetic disorders: Support groups and advocacy. *Families in Society* 74:213–21.

Weiss, J. O., B. A. Bernhardt, and N. W. Paul, eds. 1984. *Genetic Disorders and Birth Defects in Families and Society: Toward Interdisciplinary Understanding.* White Plains, N.Y.: March of Dimes Birth Defects Foundation.

Weiss, J. O., J. E. Karkalits, K. K. Bishop, and N. W. Paul, eds. 1986. *Genetic Support Groups: Volunteers and Professionals as Partners.* White Plains, N.Y.: March of Dimes Birth Defects Foundation.

White, B. J., and E. J. Madara. 1992. *The Self-Help Sourcebook: Finding and Forming Mutual Aid Self-Help Groups.* 4th ed. Denville, N.J.: American Self-Help Clearinghouse.

Annotated Bibliography

Support Groups and Group Dynamics

The materials in this list, compiled with assistance from the National Center for Education in Maternal and Child Health (NCEMCH), focus on support groups and include items on how to organize, maintain, and find them. Items may be obtained from the sources cited.

Clark, T., and M. Hughes. *Sickle Cell Mutual Help Groups; a Five-Year Study: Information, Findings, and Resources.* Chapel Hill, N.C.: Comprehensive Sickle Cell Center, Duke University, and University of North Carolina, 1992. 57 pp. Contact Psychological Research Division, University of North Carolina at Chapel Hill, 309 Battle Hill, CB#3560; (919) 966-5932. This report, prepared by the Psychological Research Division of Duke University and the University of North Carolina at Chapel Hill, provides basic materials for persons interested in organizing, conducting, and evaluating a mutual help group. It presents preliminary findings from four years of research on sickle cell mutual help groups. Section 5 of the report includes additional listings of books and articles that will provide more in-depth information.

Des Jardins, C. *How to Organize an Effective Parent/Advocacy Group and Move Bureaucracies.* Chicago: Family Resource Center on Disabilities, 1993. 270 pp. Contact Gloria Mikucki, Family Resource Center on Disabilities, 20 East Jackson Boulevard, Room 900, Chicago, IL 60604; (312) 939-3513; TDD (312) 939-3519. Book costs $12, including shipping and handling. Make check payable to Family Resource Center on Disabilities.

Hafner, D. *Learning Together: A Guide for Families with Genetic Disorders.* NMCHC B076. Rockville, Md.: U.S. Department of Health and Human Services, 1980. 24 pp. Contact National Maternal and Child Health Clearinghouse, 8201 Greensboro Drive, Suite 600, McLean, VA 22102; (703) 821-8755, ext. 254. Booklet is available at no charge. It provides information on the role of parent support groups in assisting families affected by genetic disorders. Ideas on organizing a group and possible group activities are included.

Huber, M. *Empowering Families through Self-Help Mutual Support: Training Sessions; Evaluation Report.* Albany, N.Y.: Bureau of Child and Adolescent Health, New York State Department of Health, 1992. 80 pp. Contact Bureau of Child and Adolescent Health, New York State Department of Health, Coming Tower, Room 208, Empire State Plaza, Albany, NY 12237. Price unknown. This report describes a training program that the New York State Department of Health, Bureau of Child and Adolescent Health, undertook to facilitate the development of parent-to-parent networks for children with special health needs in the health and human services system. Participants included staffs from three self-help clearinghouses and from local county health units who work in a variety of programs for children with special health needs. Topics in this report include training objectives, techniques, evaluation, follow-up activities, and a bibliography. It was funded by the Maternal and Child Health Bureau.

May, J. *Circles of Care and Understanding: Support Programs for Fathers of Children with Special Needs.* NMCHC F063. Bethesda, Md.: Association for the Care of Children's Health, 1992. 85 pp. Contact Association for the Care of Children's Health, 7910 Woodmont Avenue, Suite 300, Bethesda, MD 20814; (301) 654-6549.

Nathanson, M. N. *Organizing and Maintaining Support Groups for Parents of Children with Chronic Illness and Handicapping Conditions.* Washington, D.C: Association for the Care of Children's Health, 1986. 102 pp. Contact Association for the Care of Children's Health, 7910 Woodmont Avenue, Suite 300, Bethesda, MD 20814; (301) 654-0549. Cost is $15; for ten copies, $80.

Resnick, W. M. *The Manual for Affective Disorder Support Groups.* Baltimore: Depression and Related Affective Disorders Association, 1988. 73 pp. Contact Depression and Related Affective Disorders Association, Johns Hopkins Hospital, 600 North Wolfe Street, Meyer 3-104, Baltimore, MD 21205; (410) 955-4647. Cost is $23.81, plus $3 shipping and handling (Maryland residents add 5 percent sales tax). This manual provides an organizational framework for developing an affective disorder support group. The manual's three sections focus on the group, the leader, and the meeting. The appendix includes sample press releases, information on writing a grant application, selected lists of resources, and other useful items.

Ripley, S. *Accessing Parent Groups: A Parent's Guide.* Washington, D.C.: National Information Center for Children and Youth with Disabilities, 1993. 12 pp. Contact National Information Center for Children and

Youth with Disabilities, P.O. Box 1492, Washington, D.C. 20013; (800) 695-0285. Available at no charge.

Rosenberg, J., and D. Lee. *Perinatal Support Groups: Facilitator Training Manual.* Oakland, Calif.: Support Group Training Project, 1993. 100 pp. Contact Judith Rosenberg, Support Group Training Project, 3099 Telegraph Avenue, Berkeley, CA 94705; (510) 649-3084. Cost is $15.95, plus $3 for handling. This training manual is based on the experience of training providers from perinatal health settings in California in organizing and facilitating support groups for low-income pregnant women and new mothers. The training included a special focus on people of color. The manual covers a range of topics, including definitions, the role of a support group facilitator, the importance of caring for ourselves, core skills of support group facilitation, tips on getting started, outreach and screening, the first meeting, structure and agreements, diversity, issues in group process, methods of handling common difficulties, education and support, support groups in perinatal settings, and incentives. A checklist of topics to be covered in the group and a bibliography are included.

Swinger, B. A., ed. *Self-Help/Mutual Support Groups Resources Catalog.* Los Angeles: California Self-Help Center, 1990. 70 pp. Contact Coordinator, Public Education Service, California Self-Help Center, University of California at Los Angeles, 405 Hilgard Avenue, 2349 Franz Hall, Los Angeles, CA 90024; (213) 825-1799. Cost is $4; make check payable to the Regents of the University of California. This catalog is a guide to print and audiovisual materials for starting and maintaining mutual support groups. Topics include group leadership skills, fund-raising and grantsmanship, public relations, and resource centers. Although most materials address the consumer, there is an index of materials specifically for professionals who wish to facilitate the development of peer support groups.

Weiss, J., J. Karkalits, K. Bishop, and N. Paul, eds. *Genetics Support Groups: Volunteers and Professionals as Partners.* NMCHC B230. White Plains, N.Y.: March of Dimes Birth Defects Foundation, 1986. 182 pp. Contact National Maternal and Child Health Clearinghouse, 8201 Greensboro Drive, Suite 600, McLean, VA 22102; (703) 821-8955, ext. 254. Cost is $10.

White, B. J., and E. J. Madara, eds. *The Self-Help Sourcebook: Finding and Forming Mutual Aid Self-Help Groups.* 5th ed. Denville, N.J.: American Self-Help Clearinghouse, 1995. 272 pp. Contact American Self-Help Clearinghouse, Northwest Covenant Medical Center, Denville, NJ 07834-2995; (201) 625-7101, TDD (201) 625-9053. Cost is $9 when mailed book rate; $11 when mailed first class; prepayment required.

This directory lists national self-help groups that focus on specific life problems, including diseases and disabilities, bereavement, aging, and women's and men's concerns. It also lists clearinghouses that can help the reader identify local groups and discusses what self-help groups do and how to set one up.

Fund-Raising

Frost, G. J., ed. *Winning Grant Proposals.* University Heights, Ohio: NonProfit Partners, 1993. 160 pp. Cost is $39, plus $3.75 shipping, from NonProfit Partners, P.O. Box 18937, University Heights, OH 44118-9901.

Howe, F. *Fund-Raising and the Nonprofit Board Member.* Washington, D.C.: National Center for Nonprofit Boards, 1988. 13 pp.; cost is $4.95 from the National Center for Nonprofit Boards, 1225 19th Street, N.W., Suite 340, Washington, D.C. 20036.

Keegan, P. B. *Fundraising for Non-Profits: How to Build a Community Partnership.* New York: HarperPerennial, 1990. 215 pp.; cost is $15.

Lewis, H. L. *How to Write Powerful Fund-Raising Letters.* University Heights, Ohio: NonProfit Partners, 1993. 210 pp.; cost is $40, plus $3.75 shipping; from NonProfit Partners, P.O. Box 18937, University Heights, OH 44118-9901.

Mellon Bank Corp., Community Affairs Div. *Discover Total Resources: A Guide for Nonprofits.* Pittsburgh: Mellon Bank Corp., Community Affairs Div., 1985.

Seltzer, M. *Securing Your Organization's Future: A Complete Guide to Fundraising Strategies.* New York: Foundation Center, 1987. 514 pp.; cost is $19.95, plus $2 shipping, from the Foundation Center, 79 Fifth Avenue, New York, NY 10003.

Warwick, M. *Technology and the Future of Fundraising: The Interactive Edition.* Frederick, Md.: Aspen Publishers, 1994. 144 pp.; cost is $32, plus $4 shipping, from Aspen Publishers, P.O. Box 990, Frederick, MD 21705-9782.

Warwick, M. *Revolution in the Mailbox: How Direct Mail Fundraising Is Changing the Face of American Society.* Frederick, Md.: Aspen, 1990. 314 pp.; cost is $29.95, plus $4 shipping, from Aspen Publishers, P.O. Box 990, Frederick, MD 21705-9782.

Leadership

Aspen Publishers. *Job Descriptions for Nonprofit Board Members.* Frederick, Md.: Aspen Publishers, 1992. Fourteen camera-ready job descriptions; cost is $39 from Aspen Publishers, P.O. Box 990, Frederick, MD 21705-9782.

Barry, B. *Strategic Planning Workbook for Nonprofit Organizations.* St. Paul, Minn.: Amherst H. Wilder Foundation, 1986. 85 pages; cost is $25, plus $1 shipping, from Management Support Services, Amherst H. Wilder Foundation, 919 Lafond Avenue, St. Paul, MN 55104.

Bryson, J. *Getting Started on Strategic Planning.* San Francisco: Jossey-Bass, 1991. Two-cassette audio program. Two hours; cost is $25.95.

Houle, C. O. *Governing Boards: Their Nature and Nurture.* San Francisco: Jossey-Bass, 1989. 225 pp. Cost is $19.95, plus $1.95 shipping. Also available; *Building an Effective Nonprofit Board,* audiotape based on Houle's book. Two hours; cost is $28. Both are available from the National Center for Nonprofit Boards, 1225 19th Street, N.W., Suite 340, Washington, D.C. 20036.

Ingram, R. T. *Ten Basic Responsibilities of Nonprofit Boards.* Washington, D.C.: National Center for Nonprofit Boards, 1988. 22 pp.; cost is $4.95, from the National Center for Nonprofit Boards, 1225 19th Street, N.W., Suite 340, Washington, D.C. 20036.

Robinson, M. *Developing the Nonprofit Board.* Washington, D.C.: National Center for Nonprofit Boards, 1994. 16 pp.; cost is $4.95, from the National Center for Nonprofit Boards, 1225 19th Street, N.W., Suite 340, Washington, D.C. 20036.

Helpful Texts for Support Groups about Human Genetics

Milunsky, A. *Heredity and Your Family's Health.* Baltimore: Johns Hopkins University Press, 1992. This book offers a wealth of information on genetic risks, their potential implications, and available options; to help individuals and families become well informed about heredity.

Thompson, L. *Correcting the Code: Inventing the Genetic Cure for the Human Body.* New York: Simon and Schuster, 1994. This book explains the history and the future of human gene therapy by describing its ramifications and how those involved handled the scientific, political, and ethical problems before the first human patient could receive gene therapy.

———. *Understanding Our Genetic Inheritance. The U.S. Human Genome Project: The First Years, 1991–1995.* NIH 90-159. Bethesda: U.S. Department of Health and Human Services, and U.S. Department of Energy, 1990.

Index

Library of Congress Cataloging-in-Publication Data

Weiss, Joan O.
    Starting and sustaining genetic support groups / Joan O. Weiss and Jayne S.
Mackta.
        p.   cm.
    Includes bibliographical references and index.
    ISBN 0-8018-5023-1 (alk. paper).—ISBN 0-8018-5264-1 (pbk. : alk. paper)
    1. Genetic disorders—Patients—Services for. 2. Self-help groups. I. Mackta,
Jayne S. II. Title.
RB155.5.W45 1996
362.1'96042—dc20   95-41869